Sculpture/Inuit

Sculpture/Inuit

Sculpture of the Inuit: masterworks of the Canadian Arctic

La sculpture chez les Inuit: chefs-d'oeuvre de l'Arctique canadien

ᓴᐅᐱᒡᔭᐊᑦ ᐃᓄᐃᑦ ᓴᕐᒥᒃᐊᓄᐸᑦ ᑲᓇᑕᒥᐅᑦ ᐃᓄᐊᑦ ᓄᓇᒥ

Published for the
CANADIAN ESKIMO ARTS COUNCIL
by the
UNIVERSITY OF TORONTO PRESS

©

CANADIAN ESKIMO ARTS COUNCIL
CONSEIL CANADIEN DES ARTS ESQUIMAUX
1971
Printed in Canada
ISBN 0-8020-1846-7 *paper*
ISBN 0-8020-1845-9 *cloth*
Microfiche ISBN 0-8020-0185-8
LC 70-166937

Contents / Table des matières

Cities

1 / MOSCOW
2 / LENINGRAD
3 / COPENHAGEN
4 / PARIS
5 / LONDON
6 / PHILADELPHIA
7 / OTTAWA
8 / VANCOUVER

Communities

9 / COPPERMINE
10 / BAKER LAKE
11 / ESKIMO POINT
12 / WHALE COVE
13 / RANKIN INLET
14 / SPENCE BAY
15 / PELLY BAY
16 / ARCTIC BAY
17 / IGLOOLIK
18 / REPULSE BAY
19 / CORAL HARBOUR
20 / CLYDE RIVER
21 / PANGNIRTUNG
22 / FROBISHER BAY
23 / LAKE HARBOUR
24 / CAPE DORSET
25 / SAGLOUC (SUGLUK)
26 / POVUNGNITUK
27 / INOUCDJOUAC
(PORT HARRISON)
28 / BELCHER ISLANDS
(ILES BELCHER)
29 / POSTE-DE-LA-BALEINE
(GREAT WHALE RIVER)
30 / BELLIN (PAYNE BAY)
31 / PORT-NOUVEAU-QUÉBEC
(GEORGE RIVER)

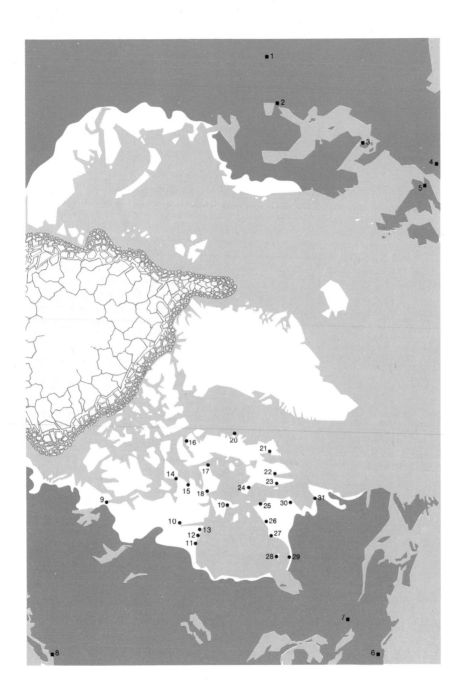

The Exhibition/L'exposition

VANCOUVER ART GALLERY, VANCOUVER

LE GRAND PALAIS, PARIS

NATIONALMUSEET, COPENHAGEN

BRITISH MUSEUM, LONDON

PUSHKIN FINE ARTS MUSEUM, MOSCOW

THE HERMITAGE, LENINGRAD

PHILADELPHIA MUSEUM OF ART, PHILADELPHIA

NATIONAL MUSEUM OF MAN, NATIONAL MUSEUMS OF CANADA, OTTAWA

Doris Shadbolt
Chairman Exhibition Committee Présidente du comité de l'exposition

James Houston, George Swinton
Consultants Conseillers

Sharon Van Raalte
Exhibition Co-ordinator Coordinatrice de l'exposition

Barbara Tyler
Committee Member Membre du comité

Luc Matter
Exhibition Designer Maquettiste de l'exposition

Tom Prescott
Exhibition Photographer Photographe de l'exposition

Foreword

In the beginning, members of the Canadian Eskimo Arts Council talked about an exhibition of 'masterworks of Eskimo sculpture.' Then each member, from the point of view of his or her unique métier, transformed a rather simplistic idea into an exhibition that embraces historical, archaeological, anthropological, and aesthetic values. The exhibition would be for people in other countries who are accustomed to seeing, owning, and living with the art of the great cultures of the world. It would give to the artists of the Canadian Arctic that world recognition which is always drawn – inexorably and magically – to the creators of the non-verbal parts of our aesthetic environment.

At last it became a full and definitive recognition of the culture of the Inuit – a people who had, down through the centuries, developed techniques of getting food, clothing, shelter, and warmth from the mammals of the arctic waters and from the birds and animals of the barren lands.

The long arctic winter nights, the life of the isolated, nomadic family, gave rise to a rich culture, essentially oral and full of myths and legends from long ago, as well as fabled and surprising events of the recent past. And it was in three dimensions because there is no tradition of flat art in the North, no books, no television screens, no paintings in the European tradition.

Here then is a cultural expression of the Inuit from the days before the white men went north of the 60th parallel; from the times of the earliest transactions between the People and the white man; and from today, a genuinely exciting time, because the artist in the Arctic gives to his people vigorous artistic expressions of a life of spirits and mythology, a life of the hunt for animals, a life of rare, precious family cohesion.

Before the spring break-up this year, the hunter-sculptor Piungituk, through Tomasie Paneepok, the interpreter, talked for hours to me about love, hate, jealousy, irony, compassion, death. He talked about forms and volumes that express moments of serenity, moments of action, moments of life or death, moments of love or not love. It was a tiny oral transaction between two cultures in a seal-skin house 75 miles from the nearest settlement. In 36 hours of conversation and seal hunting and ptarmigan shooting, we measured each other. Was the invasion of my culture weakening his? Did he see in me an exploiter? Did I see in him a 'victim' who was learning how to exploit the implicit guilt of the white man?

Finally, to make his point of humanity in search of itself, he brought out an unfinished whalebone sculpture – about a metre in height – of a woman holding her dying boy.

In that moment the gulf that separates our two cultures narrowed a little. We touched, but we did not corrupt.

Like so many of his people in the western Arctic, in the Keewatin, in the high Arctic, in the eastern Arctic, in Nouveau-Québec, Piungituk is an artist of the world: with his confident comprehension of volumes, inventiveness, feeling. All along, he has been using the language of art that is universal, the language that can bind cultures together, that can preserve a culture, the language that can strengthen a multi-cultural society without weakening or emboldening one of its members.

So with our eyes we listen to the silent language of sculpture. Listen carefully. To do otherwise – to be indifferent – is the greatest betrayal of one person by another, of one culture by another.

ACKNOWLEDGMENTS

This exhibition owes its existence to many people. There are the artists themselves, living and dead, known and unknown, who put their genius into the stone, the ivory, the whale bone, for us to see.

The Honourable Jean Chrétien, Minister of Indian Affairs and Northern Development, Government of Canada (to whom the Canadian Eskimo Arts Council volunteers its advice and counsel), has been a most patient and generous supporter of this project from the beginning. He and his senior officials – with money, wisdom, and enthusiasm – have helped to overcome problems that had never been posed before.

The Honourable Mitchell Sharp, Secretary of State for External Affairs, Government of Canada, ensured the international itinerary as part of his department's program of cultural relations with other countries and his officials in Ottawa and abroad assisted in the detailed arrangements with the various museums outside of Canada where the exhibition will be shown.

The Honourable Donald S. Macdonald, Minister of National Defence, Government of Canada, provided air transport for the exhibition throughout its North American and European itinerary.

Mr Stuart M. Hodgson, Commissioner, Government of the Northwest Territories, with characteristic generosity, both in money and man-hours, has been an important benefactor of this exhibition because so much of the art originated in the Territories.

Dr William E. Taylor, Jr, Director, National Museum of Man, Ottawa, from the outset has been an energetic and vital patron in the formation of the exhibits. We were given, not only his personal and professional knowledge of the North, but space in his Museum to work in, and invaluable day-in, day-out guidance and co-operation from his staff.

We express our grateful thanks to the officials, too numerous to mention here, of the museums in the different countries where the exhibition will be shown, without whose interest and enthusiasm the exhibition's primary purpose could not have been met.

The Canada Council gets special thanks for providing the development funds as we entered the planning stages of bringing this great collection together.

We appreciate deeply the generosity of the lenders who have agreed to let their works of art be away from home so long.

M. Marcel Evrard of the Musée de l'Homme in Paris gave to the project the benefit of his personal interest coupled with wise advice based on an exceptional range of experience in this area.

Without the efficient and dedicated work of Miss Sharon Van Raalte as Exhibition Co-ordinator, the task would never have been accomplished. Mrs Alma Houston's experience and enthusiasm for the cause was a constant source of support which we would like to acknowledge.

Mrs Doris Shadbolt, Curator of the Vancouver Art Gallery, performed her arduous task as Chairman of the Exhibition Committee with unflagging tact, faultless taste, and an unswerving zeal for excellence. Her hardworking Committee included: Miss Barbara Tyler, Chief Curator (Interpretation) of the National Museum of Man, Ottawa, and as Consultants, James Houston, designer, writer, great friend of the Northern artist, and Professor George Swinton of the University of Manitoba School of Art, writer and authority of Eskimo art. Their combined experience and expertise formed the basis on which the exhibition selection was made.

GEORGE ELLIOTT
Chairman
Canadian Eskimo Arts Council

Avant-Propos

Au début, le Conseil canadien des arts esquimaux envisageait la mise sur pied d'une exposition des 'chefs-d'oeuvres de la sculpture esquimaude.' En collaborant chacun dans l'optique de sa propre discipline, les membres du Conseil ont par la suite transformé ce simple projet en une exposition qui renferme de grandes valeurs esthétiques, historiques, archéologiques et anthropologiques. L'exposition devait s'adresser aux étrangers qui sont habitués de voir et de posséder des objets d'art provenant des grandes cultures du monde. Elle accorderait aux artistes de l'Arctique canadien cette reconnaissance qui est offerte – inexorablement et comme par magie – aux créateurs de la part non-verbale de la production esthétique dans notre milieu.

Enfin, elle devait rendre hommage à la culture des Inuit, ce peuple qui, au cours des siècles, avait élaboré des techniques lui permettant de se

nourrir, de se vêtir, de se loger et de se chauffer en utilisant les mammifères des mers arctiques, ainsi que les oiseaux et les animaux qui vivent
dans les régions désertiques du Nord.

Les longues nuits de l'hiver arctique et les moeurs de la famille isolée et
nomade ont donné lieu à une culture riche, essentiellement orale et remplie de mythes et de légendes issus des temps les plus anciens, ainsi que
d'événements suprenants et fabuleux qui se sont produits dans un passé
plus rapproché. C'était une culture à trois dimensions, car, dans le Nord,
il n'existe pas de tradition d'art unidimensionnel et il n'y a jamais eu
de livres, de téléviseurs ni même de peintures comme dans la culture
européenne.

Voici donc une histoire culturelle des Inuit, tels qu'ils étaient avant que
les Blancs ne s'aventurent au nord du 60e parallèle, tels qu'ils sont devenus
à la suite des premiers échanges avec le monde extérieur et enfin, tels
qu'ils se présentent aujourd'hui, en cette époque vraiment passionnante,
où l'artiste esquimau offre à son peuple une vision artistique de cette vie
remplie de mythes et d'esprits, centrée sur la chasse et fondée sur une
extraordinaire et précieuse cohésion familiale.

Avant la débâcle du printemps dernier, Piungituk, chasseur et sculpteur,
en compagnie de Tomasie Paneepok, l'interprète, m'a parlé pendant plusieurs heures, de l'amour, de la haine, de la jalousie, de l'ironie, de la pitié
et de la mort. Il a parlé de formes et de volumes qui expriment des
moments de sérénité, des moments d'action, des moments de vie ou de
mort, des moments d'amour ou d'aversion. Ce petit échange verbal entre
deux cultures a eu lieu dans une maison en peau de phoque à 75 milles de
l'établissement le plus proche. Pendant 36 heures consacrées à la conversation et à la chasse du phoque et du lagopède, nous nous sommes toisés.
L'incursion de ma culture affaiblissait-elle la sienne? Me considérait-il
comme un exploiteur? Est-ce que je voyais en lui une 'victime,' qui apprenait à profiter du sentiment de culpabilité de l'homme blanc?

Et puis, afin de démontrer ce qu'il entendait par l'humanité à la recherche de soi-même, il a apporté une sculpture inachevée en os de baleine,
d'environ un mètre de hauteur, représentant une forme tenant dans ses
bras son fils mourant.

A ce moment-là, l'écart qui séparait nos deux cultures s'est quelque
peu rétréci. Nous communiquions tous les deux sans pour autant changer
d'attitude.

Comme plusieurs autres Esquimaux dans l'ouest de l'archipel Arctique,
dans le Keewatin, dans l'est de l'Arctique canadien, dans le haut Arctique,

dans le Nouveau-Québec, Piungituk est un artiste universel, comme en fait foi sa compréhension assurée des volumes, de l'ingéniosité et des sentiments. Il a toujours employé le langage de l'art qui est universel, le langage qui peut relier les cultures, qui peut les préserver, qui peut consolider une société composée de plusieurs cultures, sans pour autant affaiblir ou enhardir l'une ou l'autre.

C'est pourquoi nous devons écouter avec nos yeux le langage silencieux de la sculpture. Il faut écouter attentivement. Une attitude d'indifférence entre personnes ou entre cultures est un acte de la plus haute trahison.

REMERCIEMENTS

Plusieurs personnes ont travaillé à la mise sur pied de cette exposition. Il y a d'abord les artistes, ceux qui vivent et ceux qui ont vécu, ceux qui sont connus et ceux qui ne le sont pas, ceux qui ont insufflé leur génie dans la pierre, l'ivoire ou l'os de baleine afin que nous puissions l'apprécier.

L'honorable Jean Chrétien, ministre des Affaires indiennes et du Nord canadien dans le gouvernement central (auprès de qui le Conseil canadien des arts esquimaux agit en qualité de conseiller), a fait preuve d'une grande bienveillance à l'égard du projet dès sa conception. Grâce à l'argent qu'ils nous ont donné et grâce à leur sagesse et à leur enthousiasme, M. Chrétien et ses hauts fonctionnaires ont aidé à surmonter des difficultés qui ne s'étaient jamais présentées auparavant.

L'honorable Mitchell Sharp, secrétaire d'Etat aux Affaires extérieures, a veillé, au nom du gouvernement fédéral, à l'établissement de l'itinéraire international, dans le cadre du programme de relations culturelles avec l'étranger mis en oeuvre par son ministère; ses agents à Ottawa et à l'étranger ont aidé à régler les questions de détails avec les différents musées qui accueilleront l'exposition en dehors du Canada.

L'honorable Donald S. Macdonald, ministre de la Défense nationale du Canada, a pourvu aux besoins du transport aérien pour l'exposition, tant en Amérique du Nord qu'en Europe.

Avec sa générosité habituelle en matière d'argent et de temps, M. Stuart M. Hodgson, commissaire du Gouvernement des Territoires du Nord-Ouest, s'est révélé un des principaux bienfaiteurs de cette exposition, puisque la majorité des oeuvres d'art proviennent des Territoires.

M. William E. Taylor, Jr, directeur du Musée national de l'Homme à Ottawa, s'est montré dès le début un conseiller énergique dans la mise sur pied de l'exposition. Non seulement nous a-t-il fait profiter de ses con-

naissances personnelles et professionnelles sur le Nord, mais en nous prê-
tant des locaux dans son musée, il nous a permis de tirer profit de l'appui
et des précieux conseils que son personnel nous a dispensés tout au long
du projet.

Nous exprimons notre gratitude aux directeurs, dont la liste serait ici
trop longue, des différents musées qui ouvriront leurs portes à l'exposition
et qui, par leur enthousiasme et leur dévouement, ont permis d'atteindre
le but principal visé par cette exposition.

Nous remercions tout spécialement le Conseil des Arts de nous avoir
donné les fonds nécessaires à l'organisation de cette grande collection.

Nous remercions également tous ceux qui ont si généreusement prêté
leurs oeuvres d'art et ont accepté de s'en séparer pendant si longtemps.

M. Marcel Evrard, du Musée de l'Homme à Paris, a fourné au projet
son intérêt personnel et les sages conseils que lui a dictés son expérience
exceptionnelle dans le domaine.

La tâche n'aurait pas pu être réalisée sans le travail efficace et dévoué
de Mlle Sharon Van Raalte, coordinatrice de l'exposition. Mme Alma
Houston fut une source constante d'encouragement, grâce à son expérience et à son enthousiasme.

Mme Doris Shadbolt, conservatrice de la Vancouver Art Gallery et présidente du comité de l'exposition, s'est acquittée de son rôle en faisant
preuve du plus grand tact, d'un goût certain et d'un zèle inébranlable pour
l'excellence. Les membres assidus de son comité étaient, notamment: Mlle
Barbara Tyler, conservatrice en chef du Musée national de l'Homme à
Ottawa et, en tant que conseillers, M. James Houston, créateur, écrivain et
grand ami de l'artiste du Nord, et M. George Swinton, professeur à l'Ecole
d'art de l'Université du Manitoba, écrivain et expert en art esquimau.
Leur expérience et leurs grandes connaissances ont été utiles dans le choix
des pièces d'exposition.

GEORGE ELLIOTT
président
Conseil canadien des arts esquimaux

ᓯᕗᓕᒋ

ᐱᒋᐊᓂᒐᓂ, ᑕᑯᐊ ᑲᒪᔪᑦ ᑲᓇᑕᒥᐅ ᐃᓄᐃ ᑎᑎᕋᔭᓯᒪᔪᓕᕆᔪᒋᑦ ᐅᑲᐅᓯᑲᓚᐅᒪᑕ ᑕᑯᔭᓴᓂ "ᐊᒋᓗᐊᓂᒋᓂᒃ ᐱᓇᓯᑕᐱᓂᓂ ᐃᓄᓄᑦ ᓴᓇᐅᒐᓂ". ᑕᐃᒪ ᐊᕋᓂ ᑲᒪᔪᑦ, ᑕᑯᓴᐅᑎᓯᓚᐅᕋ ᐊᔾᒋᒋᕋᓂ ᓴᓇᓯᒪᔪᐃᑦ ᐊᑭᓯᒪᓂᒋᓂ, ᐱᐅᓂᓴᓂ ᐱᒐᓚᐅᕋ ᑕᑯᓴᒧᑎᓯᒋ ᐱᐅᔪᓇᐅᓂᒋ ᐅᕙᓯᐊᕈᓂᑕᐃ ᐊᑯᓂᓂᑕᐃᑦ, ᑲᐅᔾᒐᓯᐊᑕᐅᓂᒋ, ᐃᓗᓇᓚᒪᒋ ᓯᓇᕋᐃᓇᐃ, ᐊᒪᓗ ᐱᐅᔪᓂᒋᑦ. ᑕᑯᐊ ᑕᑯᔭᓴᐃ ᐱᔭᐅᔪᓴᐅᓗᑎ ᕿᓇᕋᐃᓇᑯᓄ ᐊᓯᐊᓂ ᓄᓇᓚᓄ ᑕᑯᓄᒐ ᑕᑯᔪᓄᑦ, ᓇᒥᓂᑲᕋᓂ ᐊᒪᓗ ᐃᓄᓯᑲᑲᑎᑲᕋᓂ ᓴᓇᓯᒪᔪᓂ ᐊᒋᔪᓂ ᓴᓇᓯᒪᔪᓂ ᓯᓚᔪᐊᒥ. ᕋᓂᔭᐅᑲᔭᒪᑕ ᑕᑯᓄᒐ ᑎᑎᕋᔭᑎᒋᓄ ᑲᓇᑕᒥᐅᑦ ᐃᓄᐃᑦ ᓄᓇᒐᓂ ᐃᒪᓇ ᓯᓚᔪᐊᒥ ᐃᓚᑕᓇᑲᐃᒪᑕ ᑕᐃᒪᒐ ᑎᑎᕆᓯᒪᓂᒐ ᐊᔾᔪᐊᑦ — ᐱᔪᒪᔭᐅᓂᒋ ᐊᒪᓗ ᐊᔪᒐᐃᓂᒋ — ᓴᓇᔭᐅᔪᓇᕋ ᑎᑎᕆᓯᒪᒋᓗᑎ ᐃᓚᒋᔭᐅᓗᑎ ᐱᐅᓴᓂᑎᓄ.

ᑎᑭᐅᑎᓴᕆᑕᑯ ᐃᓗᓇᒋ ᐊᒪᓗ ᐊᑭᓯᐊᓯᑎ ᐃᓚᑕᓇᑲᐃᓂᒐ ᐱᐅᓯᒋᓂ ᐃᓄᐃ — ᕿᓇᕋᐃᓇᑯᓄ ᐃᓄᓯᒪᓚᕋᓄ ᐊᕆᔪᐃ ᐊᒥᓯ ᓇᓯᒋ, ᐱᔭᓇᑎᔪᓇᓯᓯᒋ ᑲᐅᔾᒪᓂᒥᓄ ᓂᑭᑕᑲᑕᓗᑎ, ᐊᓄᕆᓂ, ᐱᐅᓂᓴᒥᓚᓗᑎ, ᐊᒪᓗ ᓂᕈᒥᕋᒥᒃ ᐃᒪᑲᓚᓗᑎ ᐃᓄᐃᑦ ᓄᓇᒐᑕ ᐃᒪᒋᓂ ᐱᔭᓂ ᐊᒪᓗ ᑯᐸᓄᐊ ᑎᒥᐊᓂ ᐅᒪᔭᓂ ᐱᔪᕕᐅᒋᕋᓂ ᓄᓇᓂ.

ᐊᑯᓂᐊᓗ ᐃᓄᐃᑦ ᓄᓇᒐ ᐅᓄᐊᒍᑲᑕᕋ ᐅᑭᐅᑯ, ᐃᓄᓯᒋ ᕿᓇᑯᑕᑲᒋᕋᒥᓗᑎ, ᑲᓄᑭᐊ ᐃᓚᒋᓗᑎ ᐊᒋᓚᑲᑕᕋ ᐱᐅᔪᒥ ᐱᕈᓯᒪᓂᑲᓗᑎ, ᐃᓚᒋᓯᐊᓂᒋ ᐅᑲᓯᒪᓗᑎ ᐊᒪᓗ ᐃᓗᓇᒋ ᐊᕋᐸᑕᕕᓂᒋ ᐊᒪᓗ ᐅᓂᑲᐅᓯ ᑕᐃᓯᒪᓂᐊᓗᓂᑕᐃᑦ, ᑕᐃᒪᓇᑕᐅ ᓯᓚᒋᓂᒋ ᐅᓂᑲᐅᓯ ᐊᔪᒐᐃᓇᓗᑎᓗ ᑲᓄᐃᒍᓯᕕᓂᓂ ᒪᓇᑕᒐ ᐊᕋᕋᕕᓂᓂ. ᐊᒪᓗ ᐱᒐᓯᓯᒪᔪ ᐅᕋᓯᒋᑦ ᐅᑲᓯᒪᔪᑲᓂᒋᒪ ᐅᓂᑲᐅᓯᓂ ᑎᑎᕋᔭᓯᒪᔪᓂ ᐃᓄᐃ ᓄᓇᒐᓂ, ᐅᑲᓚᒪᑲᒐᓂ, ᑕᓚᕕᑲᒐᓂᓗ ᑕᐅᕋᒐᓇᓂ ᑎᑎᕋᔭᓯᒪᔪᑲᒋ ᓯᓂ ᐃᐅᑎᐱᒥ ᐅᑲᓯᒪᔪᓂ.

ᑕᕙᓂ ᑕᐃᒪ ᐃᓄᐃᑦ ᐱᐅᓯᒋ ᐅᑲᓯᒪᔫ ᐱᒋᐊᓯᑎ ᑕᐃᓯᒪᓂ ᑲᓗᓇᒥ ᐃᓄᐃᑦ ᓄᓇᒐᓄᕋᑲᓚᐅᑎᓇᔪ: ᑕᐃᓯᒪᓂᐅ ᑎᓗᔪ ᐱᒋᐊᓯᔪᐱᓂ ᐱᓇᓯᐊᑲᑕᐅᑎᒋᐊᓯᓯᑎ ᐃᓄᐃᑦ ᑲᓗᓇᓗ, ᐊᒪᓗ ᒪᓇᐅᓚᕋ, ᐊᒃᓯᐊᓗ ᑯᐱᐊᓯᓂᑲᓚᕋ, ᑎᑎᕋᔭᑎ

ᐃᓄᐃᑦ ᓄᓇᓕᓂ ᑐᓂᓯᑲᑕᓚᒪᑕ ᐃᓄᑲᑎᒥᓄ ᓯᒍᔪᓂ ᑎᑎᑐᔭᑎ ᐅᑲᓯᒪᔪᓚᐅᑲᑕᓚᒪᑕ ᐃᓄᐃ ᐃᓄᓯᕆᓂ ᐊᒪᓗ ᐅᓂᑲᐅᓯᓂ, ᐃᓄᓯᕆᓂ ᐊᒍᓇᓯᐊᓯᑎ ᐅᒪᔪᓂ, ᐃᓄᓯᕆᓂ ᓯᕆᐅᓇᐃᑐᒥ, ᐱᓯᐊᑲᑕᐅᑎᔪᓂ ᑭᑐᓕᕆ ᐃᓚᕆᓯᐊᓂᓕᓂ.

ᐅᐱᓕᑯᑦ ᓯᑯᐃᓚᐅᑎᓇᒍ ᒪᓇ ᐅᑭᐅᒃ, ᐊᒍᓇᓯᐊᑎ ᓴᓇᓯᒪᔭᐅᔪ ᐱᐅᕆᑐᒧ, ᑐᓴᔭᑎᒍ ᑕᒧᓯ ᐸᓂᐳᒃ ᐅᑲᐅᓯᑎᔭᐅᓚᐅᑐ ᐃᑲᐅᓂᓂ ᐊᒥᓯᓂ (ᐅᐸᓄ) ᐅᑲᐅᓯᑲᓯᓂ ᓇᓚᓂᐅ ᒥᓴᓄ, ᐅᒥᓯᓂᒥ, ᐱᔭᑐᓴᓂᒥ, ᐅᓂᑲᓂᒥ, ᑐᑯᓂᒥ. ᑕᓇ ᐅᑲᐅᓯᑲᓚᐅᑐ ᐊᑭᓯᒪᓂᐅᑉ ᒥᓴᓄ ᐊᒪᓗ ᐱᓇᓯᓂᒥ ᐃᒪᓇ ᐅᓕᓗᓂ ᒪᓇᓂᑕᒥ ᓂᑕᓯᐊᑐᓂ ᒪᓇᓂᑕᒥᒃ ᑲᓄᐃᒍᑕᐅᔪᒥ, ᒪᓇᓂᑕᒥ ᐃᓄᓯᒥ ᐅᐸᓗᓂ ᑐᑯᓂᒥ, ᒪᓇᓂᑕᒥ ᓇᓚᓂᒥ ᐅᐸᓗᓂ ᓇᓚᓂᐅᕆᑐᒥ. ᒥᑭᑐᑯᓗᓚᐅᑐ ᐅᑲᓯᒪᓂᓕᑕ ᐱᕆᐊᓯᒪᓂᓕ ᑕᑯᓄᓕ ᒪᕈᓄ ᓴᓇᓯᒪᔪᓄ ᓇᓯᐅᑉ — ᑭᓯᕆᓄ ᐃᒃᑐᒧ 75 ᐅᓕᓯᓂᓚ ᐱᕆᐊᓯᓂ ᑲᓂᓂᐸᒧᑦ ᐃᒃᑐᑕᓚᒧ. 36 ᓂ ᐃᑲᐅᓂᓂ ᐅᑲᑲᑎᕆᓚᐅᑐᒍ ᓇᓯᓯᐅᓂᒥ ᐊᒪᓗ ᐊᑭᕆᓂ ᓯᕆᐊᑲᑕᓂᒥ, ᐅᑐᕋᐅᑎᓚᐅᒃ ᑐᒍ. ᐃᓯᒪᓚᐅᓕᒪ ᐱᐅᓯᑎᔭᓂ ᑕᓯᒪ ᐱᐅᓯᓕ ᓯᑯᑎᓚᐅᐸᕋ ? ᑕᑯᓚᐅᐸ ᐅᐸᓂ ᓯᓂᑎᔭᓂ ? ᑕᑯᓚᐅᐸᕋ ᑕᓇ "ᓴᓚᓂᑎᓗᒍ" ᑕᓇ ᐃᓚᓂᐊᓚᐅᑐ ᑲᓄ ᓯᓂᑎᔭᒥ ᐊᐱᑎᕆᓯᒍ ᑕᑯᓂᓕ ᒪᕈᓂᕆᓂ ᑲᓗᓇ ᐃᓄᐃᓗ ?.

ᑐᑭᑕᓴᕋᑕᓚᐅᑐ, ᐅᑲᓕᓯᑕᒥᓂ ᑲᓄᐃᑐᓂᓕᑕ ᑭᓂᑕᐅᓂᓕ ᐃᒥᓄ, ᑕᓇ ᓄᐃᓯᓚᐅᑐ ᐱᔭᑎᓯᒪᕆᑐᒥ ᑭᓚᓗᓕᐅᑉ ᓴᐅᓂᓕᓂ ᓴᓇᓯᒪᔪᒥ — ᑕᑭᓂᓕ ᐅᑐᕋᓯᒪᓗᓂ — ᐊᒃᓇ ᑎᒍᒥᐊᑐᒃ ᑐᑯᓂᐅᔭᑐᒥ ᐃᒃᓂᒥᓂ.

ᑕᐃᓯᒪᓂᐅᑎᓗᒍ ᐃᓚᓕᓂ ᐊᕕᑎᓯᓚᐅᑐ ᒪᕈᓂ ᓴᓇᓯᒪᔪᓂ ᒥᑭᑐᑯᓗᒥ ᑐᑭᑲᓚᓗᓂ. ᐊᑐᐃᓗᓄ, ᐃᓚ ᓯᑯᒥᓯᓚᐅ ᕆᑐᒍ.

ᐃᒪᓇ ᐊᒥᓯᐊᓗᐃᑦ ᐃᓄᑲᑎᕆ ᑭᑕᓂᒥᐅ ᐃᓄᐃᑦ ᓄᓇᓕᓂ ᑭᐳᐊᑕᒥᐅᓗ, ᐃᓄᐃᓗ ᓄᓇᒪᑎᓕᓂᒥᐅᑦ, ᐅᑯᒥᐅᓗ ᑯᐱᒃᒥᐅᓗ ᐃᓄᐃ ᓄᓇᓕᓂ. ᐱᐅᕆᑐ ᓴᓇᒍᐊᑎᐳ ᓯᓚᔪᐊᒥ: ᓯᒍᔪᒥ ᐅᐱᓇᓗᓂ ᐊᒃᓯᐊᓗ ᐃᓯᒪᑲᓂᒥᓄ ᓴᓇᓗᓂ. ᑲᐅᔭᒪᔭᒥᓂ, ᐃᒃᐱᒍᓯᓕᒥ. ᑕᐃᒪᓕᓂᐊᓗ ᑕᓇ ᐊᑐᑎᓯᒪᔪ ᐅᑲᐅᓯᓕᓂ ᓴᓇᓂᐅᑉ ᐱᔭᑎᐊᑲᓗᐊᓂᓕᓂ, ᐅᑲᐅᓯ ᐊᑕᓯᒍᓇᒪ ᓴᓇᓯᒪᔪᐃᑦ ᑲᑎᓯᕆ, ᐱᓯᒪᔭᐅᒍᓇᓗᑎ ᓴᓇᓯᒪᔪ. ᐅᑲᐅᓯ ᐊᑭᓯᒪᑎᓯᒍᓇᒪ ᐊᒥᓯᓂ ᓴᓇᓯᒪᔪᓂ ᓯᑯᑎᕆ ᓗᕆ ᐅᐸᓗᓂ ᐱᔪᓇᓯᑎᓗᕆ.

ᑕᐃᒪ ᐱᔭᑎᓄ ᓇᓚᐳᒍᑦ ᓂᐱᑲᕆᑐᒥ ᐅᑲᐅᓯᒥ ᓴᓇᓯᒪᔪᒥ. ᓇᓚᓯᐊᑎᓯ ᐊᓯᐊᒍᓴᕈᐊᒪ — ᐱᐅᕆᔭᐅᑎᓗᕆᑦ — ᐊᕆᓂᐸᐅᒪ ᑲᐅᔭᔭᐅᓂᓕ ᐊᑕᐅᓯᒧ ᐃᓄᒃᒧ ᐊᓯᐊᓄ ᐃᓄᒥᔪᒧ, ᓇᓚᕆᓄ ᐱᐅᓯᐅᑉ ᐊᓯᐊᓄ.

ᑎᑎᕋᑕᐅᓯᒪᓂᕆ

ᑕᓇ ᑕᑯᔭᓴ ᐊᑭᓂᓴᑕᑎᔭᐅᓚᐅᑐ ᐊᒥᓯᓄ ᑭᓇᑐᐃᓇᑯᓄ. ᑕᐃᑲᓂ ᓴᓇᒍᐊᑎᓯᔭᑲᓚᐅᒪ ᐃᒥᓄᑐᓂ, ᐃᓄᓯᒥ ᐊᒪᓗ ᑐᑯᓂᒥ, ᑲᐅᔭᒪᓇᑐᓂ ᑲᐅᔭᒪᓇᕆᑐᓂᓗ. ᑭᓇᑯ ᐃᓚᔭᓂᒪᓕᑕ ᓴᓇᔭᕕᓂᒥᓂ ᐅᔭᕋᒥ, ᑐᓕᓂ, ᑭᓚᓗᓕᐅᑉ ᓴᐅᓂᓕᓂ ᐅᐸᑎᓄ ᑕᑯᔭᓴᐅᑎᓗᕆ.

Hon. Jean Chretien ᐊᓕᔪᑲᓕ ᐃᓄᓚᑎᔭᑯᓄ ᑲᐸᒪᑯᒥᐅ ᑲᓇᑕᒥ, (ᑕᑯᓂᓕ ᑲᓇᑕᒥᐅᓂ ᐃᓄᐃ ᓴᓇᒍᐊᓕᕆᓂ ᑲᒪᔭᓂ ᐃᑲᔪᓚᐅᑐ ᐅᑲᑎᐅᓗᓂ ᐊᒪᓗ ᐊᐅᓚᓯᔭᐅᓗᓂ) ᐱᓯᐊᑐᒪᑎᐊᓗᓚᐅᑐ ᐃᑲᔪᓯᐊᓯᓂ ᐃᑲᔪᑎᐊᓚᓂ ᑕᓯᒪ ᐊᑭᑕᐅᓚᓂᐊᓂᓕᑕ ᐱᕆᐊᓂᓕᓂ. ᑕᓇ ᐊᒪᓗ ᐃᑐᓂᓴᐃ ᐃᑲᓇᐃᔭᑐᑯᑎᕆ — ᑭᓇᐅᔭᒧ, ᐊᑭᓚᐅᑐ, ᐊᒪᓗ ᐃᓯᒪᑲᓯᐊᓚᐅᑐ — ᐃᑲᔪᓗᑎ ᐊᑲᐅᕆᒍᑕᐅᔪᓂ ᐊᓂᒍᑎᓯᓗᑎ ᑕᐃᒪᓇ ᐊᑲᐅᕆᒍᑕᐅᓚᐅᓯᒪᕆᑐᓂ ᐊᓯᐊᒍ.

Hon. Mitchell Sharp, ᑎᑎᕋᑎᐅᔪ ᑕᑯᔭᓴᓚᑎᔭᑯᓄ, ᑲᐸᒪᒥ ᑲᓇᑕᒥ, ᐊᑕᓇᐃᓚᑎᓯᒪᔪ ᐃᓗᓇᕆᓄ ᐊᐅᓚᑲᑕ ᕆᐊᓴ ᐃᓚᕆᔭᐅᓗᑎ ᑕᓯᒪ ᐱᓇᓯᕕᓕᑕ ᐱᓇᓯᓂᓕᓄ ᐊᕆᓚᐸᓚᐊᓂᓕᑕ ᐃᓚᕆᔭᐅᓂᓕᓄ ᐱᑲᑎᑲᓗᓂ ᐊᓯᕆᓂ ᓄᓇᓂ ᐊᒪᓗ ᐃᑲᓇᐃᔭᑐᑯᑎᕆ ᐊᑐᒍᐊᒥ ᐊᒪᓗ ᓄᓇᐃᑦ ᐊᓯᐊᓂ ᐃᑲᔪᓗᓂ ᐊᑭᑲᑕᓯᓂ ᑕᑯᓂᓕ ᐊᒥᓯᓂ ᑭᒥᕈᐊᕕᓂ ᑲᓇᑕᐅᑉ ᓯᓚᑕ ᓂᑐᓂᒃ ᑕᑯᔭᓴᓂ ᑕᑯᔭᑐᕕᐅᓚᐅᑐᒃ.

Hon. Donald S. Macdonald, ᐊᓕᔪᑲ ᑲᓄᑐᐃᓇ ᐃᐱᒍᓯᓂᒧ, ᑲᐸᒪᒥ ᑲᓇᑕᒥ, ᑕᓇ ᐃᑲᔪᓚᐅᑐ ᑲᓕᑕᓯᑯᑦ ᐃᕆᕋᔪᓂ ᑕᑯᔭᓴᐅᓗᑎ ᑕᐳᓕᓚᒪ ᐊᒥᐊᑎᑲᐃ ᓄᓇᓕᑕ ᑕᕋᓄ ᐊᒪᓗ ᐃᐅᑎᐱᐅ ᓄᓇᓕᓄᑲᑕᑐᓂ.

Stuart M. Hodgson, ᐊᓕᔪᑲ ᐃᓯᒪᑕ ᐃᓄᐃᑦ ᓄᓇᓕᑕ ᑲᐸᒪᓕᓄ ᓄᓇᓯᐊᒧ, ᑎᑎᕋᓯᒪᔪᓄ ᐃᑲᔪᒍᒪᓗᓂ. ᑕᒪᑭᓄ ᑭᓇᐅᔭᒧ ᐊᒪᓗ ᐱᓇᓯᑐᐃ ᐃᑲᐅᓂᕆᓄ, ᐊᒃᓯᐊᓗ ᐱᔭᑎᐊᑲᓯᒪᒪ ᐱᓯᐊᓂᕆ ᑕᓯᒥᓕ ᐊᒃᓯᐊᓗ ᓴᓇᒍᐊᓕᐅᑉ ᐱᕆᐊᓂᓕᓄ ᐃᓄᐃᑦ ᓄᓇᓕᓂ ᓄᓇᓯᐊᒥ.

Dr William E. Taylor, Jr ᐊᓕᔪᑲ, ᐃᓗᓇᕆᓄ ᑭᒥᕈᐱᒥ ᐅᐸᓯᐊᒍᓂᑕᓂ ᐊᑐᒍᐊᒥ ᐱᕆᐊᓯᓂ ᐊᒃᓯᐊᓗ ᐱᔭᑎᐊᑲᓯᒪᔪ ᐊᒪᓗ ᐱᔭᑎᐊᑲᒪᑎᑐ ᐃᑲᔪᓯᓯᒪᒪ ᑕᐃᒪᓇ ᐊᑭᑕᐅᓂᓕ ᑕᑯᔭᓴᐃ. ᑐᓂᔭᐅᓚᐅᑐᒍ, ᐃᒥᓂᓗᑎᕆᑐ ᐊᒪᓗ ᑲᓄᑐᐃᓇ ᑲᐅᔭᒪᓂᓕᓄ ᐃᓄᐃ ᓄᓇᓕᓂ, ᐃᓚ ᐃᓂᑲᑐ ᑭᒥᕈᕕᒥᓂ ᐱᓇᓯᐱᓴᒥ, ᐊᒪᓗ ᐊᑐᐃᓇᑲᑲᑕᓗᓂ ᐅᒃᓗᐃ ᐃᓚᕆᓂ, ᐅᒃᓗᓗ ᓇᒪᑲᓕᔭᑲᓗᓂ ᐊᒪᓗ ᐃᑲᔪᑎᑲᓗᓂ ᑕᑯᓂᓕ ᐱᓇᓯᑎᒥᓂ.

ᑯᔭᓇᒥᐳᒍᑦ ᐊᒃᓯᐊᓗ ᐃᑲᓇᐃᔭᑎᓂᒃ, ᐊᒪᓗ ᐊᒥᓯᓂ ᐅᑲᑕᐅᔪᓂᒃ ᑕᒪᓂ ᑕᑯᔭᑐᑯᕕᓂ ᓄᓇᓂ ᑕᐃᑲᓂ ᑕᑯᔭᓴᓂ ᑕᑯᔭᑐᕕᐅᓚᐅᑐᓂ, ᐱᑕᑲᑎᓇᕆ ᑕᑯᐊ ᐱᐅᓴᑐ ᐊᒪᓗ ᑯᕕᐊᕆᔭᑲᑐ ᑕᑯᔭᓴᐃᑦ ᓯᐳᓚᐸᒍᒍᑕᐅᒪᑕ ᑲᑎᒍᑕᐅᒍᓇᓕᔭᓂᕆᑐᑦ.

ᑲᓇᑕᒥ ᓴᓇᒍᐊᓕᓚᑎᔭᑦ ᑯᔭᓇᒥᒍᑎᑲᓚᐅᑐ ᐃᑲᔪᓂᒥᓄ ᐊᕆᓚᑎᓯᕆᐊᓴ ᐃᓚᕆᔭᐅᒍᑎᕆᓚᐅᑕᑎᓂ ᑕᑯᔭᓴᓚᐅᓚᓂᐊ ᑐᓄ ᑕᓇ ᑎᑭᑎᓯᓚᐅᑐ ᐊᕆᔪᓂ ᓄᐊᓯᓂᒥ ᑲᑎᓯᓯᓂ.

ᓇᑯᓴᐳᒍᑦ ᑯᕕᐊᓯᐳᒍᑦ ᐊᒃᓯᐊᓗ ᐃᑲᔪᒍᒪᓚᐅᒪᑕ ᐊᓕᔪᑲᓂ ᑕᐃᑯᓂᓕ ᐊᕆᓚᐅᑐᓂ ᐊᐅᓚᑎᑕᐅᓚᐅᒪᑕ ᐱᓇᓯᓂᒧ ᐊᐅᓚᓯᒪᓗᑎ ᐊᓇᕋᒥᓂ ᐊᑯᓂᐊᓗᒃ.

M. Marcel Evrard ᗰᕈᐸᑉᓄᑦᓄ ᐊᑦᓴᓄᑦᓄ ᐱᒥᐳᐱᕟᐅ ᒍᓄᑕᐃᑐᐅ Cᑦᓵᕐᒪᓗᓂ ᐃᑉᒌᓄ ᐊᒥᓄ ᐱᐅᑕᓄ
ᖕᓄ ᐃᓕᕐᐅᑎᑕᓄ ᐃᑉᒪᑉᕐᐊᐅᒍᒐᓪ ᑉᒪᕐᒐᒐ ᐁᓗᐅᑕᓴᓂᒻ ᐦᒐ ᕐᐅᑐᓄ Cᐊᒪᕐᖃᐃᑕᑉᕐᐃ ᑐᓄᐳᑐᒻ Cᐃᑉᕙ ᓴᐊᕐᒻ.

ᖕᖃᑐ ᓄᑦᓂᕐᒻ ᐊᒪᓗ ᐱᓴᒍᐊᓄ ᐱᕐᓄᓄ ᐱᓴᕐᑐᑉᕐᑦᑦ Miss Sharon Van Raalte Cᑐᕐᓄᒐ ᐃᑉᒌᑉᕐ ᑉᒪᑕᑉᒪᒪ, ᖕᐊᒐᐅᓴ ᖕᐱᕟᑉᐊᒍᐊᒍᓗᐁᑉᕐᑐ ᑉᒪᑉᕐᑦᑦ Mrs Alma Houston ᐊᑉᑦ ᑉᒪᕟᒍᒪ ᐊᒪᓗ ᑉᒪᕟᒪᑉᓄᒪᓄ ᐊᑉᕐᒪᒐᑉᑉᕐᑐ ᑉᓄᐊᓄᕐᑦᕐ ᖕᐱᕟᐊᑉᓄᕟᑉᕐᑦᓂᓄ ᑉᒪᕈᒪᒪᑉᓄᒪᓄ.

Mrs Doris Shadbolt ᐊᒪᐅᑉ ᑉᐅ ᑉᒌᑉᑦ ᐱᒥᐊᒪᒐᒐᓄ, ᑉᒪᕟᒪᒐᑉᑉᑦ ᐊᑉᑐᒍᑉᐊᔪᕐᑉ ᖕᐊᕐᕐᓄ ᐊᒪᐅᑉᒍᒐᒐ Cᑐᒪᓗ Cᑐᕐᐅᖕᑉᕟᕈᑉᑐᒻ ᖕᐱᕐᕿᑉᐊᐅᑉᕐ ᐊᒐᕐᒍᐊᕈᒪ, Cᒪᕐᕈᐊᕐᓄ ᑐᑮᕐᓄ, ᐊᒪᓗ ᑉᒪᐊᐅᓄᕟᕐᒃ ᐊᑉᕐᐊᓄᑉ ᖕᑉᐊᑉᑦᑦ. ᖕᐊᕐᐊᑐᑉᒪᕟᐊᐅᓄᒪᓪ CᑐᕐᓄᕟᐊᑉᑉᕈᑉCᐳᑉᓂ: ᑉᒪᕟᐳᑉᓄ, James Houston ᐊᑉᕐᐊᐅᑉ, ᕟᕟᕈᕟ, ᐊᑉᕐᐊᒐ ᐱᑉᕟᑉᕙᑉᕈ ᐃᐅᐅᑦ ᓴᐊᑉC ᕟᕟᐳᕐᓄᕟᒪᓄ, ᐊᒪᓗ ᕐᐊᐃᐊᐅ ᐃᑕᐅᐊᕐᕈᑉᕐ George Swinton, ᐃᑕᐅᐊᕐᕿᐊᑉᕈ ᒪᐅᑉᕈᑦ ᕟᕟᐳᕐᓄ ᐃᑕᐅᐊᑉᓄ, ᕟᕟᕈᕟ ᐊᒪᓗ ᑉᒪᕟᐳᑉᓄ ᐃᐅᐅᑦ ᕟᕟᐳᕐᕟᓄ, Cᑉᑉ ᐃᑉᐳᑉ Cᐳᑉᕐ ᑉᒪᕟᕈᓄᕟ ᐊᒪᓗ ᑉᒪᕟᕈᓄᕟᑉ ᐊᑉᕈᕈᓄᕟ Cᑉᑉ Cᑐᕐᓄᐊᑉ ᓄᑉᐊᑉᑐᕟᕈᑉ ᐊᑉᑉᑉᐅᑉᑉᕐ: ᐊᒪᓗ Miss Barbara Tyler, ᐊᒪᐅᑉ ᑉᒪᕟᐳᑉᓄ (ᑐᑉᑐᑉᑦᓄᕟᐊᑉᕈᓄ) ᕐᐊᑐᐃᐊᐅᑉ ᐱᒥᑐᐃᕟ Cᑐᕐᓄᑉᐊᕟ ᐊᑉᑉᕟ.

George Elliott
ᐊᒪᐅᑉᑉ
ᑉᐊCᕟᑉᑦ ᐃᐅᐊᑉ ᖕᐊᒍᐊᑉᑉᕟᕐᑉᕟᕟ

Sivuligit

pigianingit, takua kamajiit kanatamiut Inuit tititujasimajulirijigiit ukau-
sikalaumata takujasanik 'angiluaninginik pinasutavininik Inunut sanau-
ganik.' Taima atuni kamajiit, takusautisilautu ajigingitunik sanasimajuit
aqisimaninginik, piunisanik pingasilautu takusamutisugit piugunaunigit
uvasiarunitiit akuninitaiit, qaujigasuatauningit, ilunalimangit sunatui-
naiit, ammalu piujiningit. takua takujasaiit pijaujusalutik kinatuinakunut asiani nunalinut takuninga takujunut, naminikatunik ammalu Inusi-
katikatunik sanasimajunik angijunik sanasimajunik silajuami. tunijau-
gajamatatakununga tititujatinginut kanatamiut Inuit nunangani immana
silajuami ilitanakimata taimanga titirasimaninga ajiguat – pijumajauni-
git ammalu ajugainigit – sanajaugunatu titirasimalutik ilagijaulutik piu-
sanitinut.

Tikiutisarataku ilunagit ammalu aqisiasutik ilitanakaininga piusin-
ginik Inuit – kinatuinakunut Inusimalirtunut araruit amisut nasugit,

19

pijunatigunasisugit kaujimaniminut niqitakatalutik, anuranik, piunisa-
mililutik, ammalu nirumitumi imakalilutik inuit nunangata ilangini pijuni
ammalu qupanuani timianik umajuniklu piruviungitunik nunanit.

akunialu Inuit nunanga unuagukatatu ukiuku, inusingit kinakutakagi-
tumilutik, qanukia Ilagilutik angilikatatu piujumik pirusimanikalutik,
Ilagisianigit ukasimalutik ammalu Ilunangit atupataviningit ammalu
unikausi taisumanialunitaiit, taimanatau sulinginingit unikasit ajugailuna-
lutilu qanuigusivinik mannarata atutuvininik. ammalu pingasisimajut
uutusugit uqasimajukaningimat unikausinik tititujasimajunik Inuit nunangani, ukalimakagani, talavisakanganilu tautugananik tititujasimajukagi-
suni Iuripimi ukasimajunik.

tavani taima Inuit piusingit ukasimavut pigiasutik taisumani qalluna
Inuit nuna nganulautinagit taisumanialutilugu pigiasijuvinit pinasuaka-
tautingiasisutik Inuit qallunalu, ammalu manaulitu, aksualu quviasuni-
kalirtut, tititujati Inuit nunangani tunisikatlimata inukatiminu sungu-
junik tititujati ukasimajuliukatalimata Inuit inusiginik ammalu unikausinik, inusiginikangunasuasutik umajunik, inusiginik sugiunaitumik,
pisiakatautijunik qitungait Ilagininginik.

Upingaku manna ukiu, anaunasuasutik sanasimajauju piungitumut,
tusajitigut tamusie panirpuk ukausurijaulautu ikauninik amisunik (uvan-
nu) ukausikasuni nalliniup misanut, umisunimik, pijilusanikmik, unikani-
mik, mamianikmik, tukunimik. tanna ukausikalautu akisimaniup misanu
ammalu pinasunimik imanna uklunik mananitamik nitasiaunik qanuigu-
taujumik, mannanitamik inusikmik uvaluni tugunimik, mannanitamik
nalin imik uvvaluni naliniungitumik. mikitukululautuk ukasimaningata
pigiasimaninga takununga marunu sanasimajunu natsiup qisiginu ikalumu
75 ungasinilik pingiasuni qaninipamut ikalutalikmut. 36 nik ikauninik
ukakatikalautugut ammalu natssiunimik ammalu akiginik sugiakata nik-
mik, uturakatautilautugu. issumalaurama piusirijani tatsuma piusinga
sukutilaupara? takulaupaa uvanni sunirijani? takulaupangaa tanna 'sala-
nitilugu' tanna ilinialautuk qanu sunirijamik apirisuni takuninga maru-
ninginik kalluna inuitlu?

tukitasarayalautu, uka gasutaminik qanuituningata qinitauninga im-
minu, tanna nuisilautu pijarisimagitumik qilalugaup sauninganik sanasimajumik – takininga ukturasimaluni – arnna tigumiatuk tukuniujatu-
mik irniminik.

taisumaniuyilugu ilangani avitisilautu maruni sanasimajunik mikituku-
lumik tukikalilutik. attuilunu, illa sikumisilaungitugu.

immanna amisualuit inukatigit kitanimiut inuit nunangani kivuatani-
miulu, inuilu nunamaringanimiut, ukumiulu, kupikmiulu inuit nunan-

gani. piungituk sanaguatiuvuk silajuami: sugurumik uppinaluni aksualu isumakaniminu sanaluni. qaujimajamini, ipigusugami. taimanganialu tanna atutisimajuk ukausingani sananiup pijariakaluaningani, ukausi atatisigunama sanasimajut katisugit, pisimajaugunalutik sanasimajuit. kausi aqisimatisigunamat amisunik sanasimajuni sukutigilugit uvvaluni pijunasitilugit.

tiama ijitinut nalapugut nipikagitumik ukausimik sanasimajumik. nalasiarisi. asiagusaruamata – piugijaungilutik – aginipaumat kaujijauninga atausimut inumut asianut inumijumut, nalligini piusiup assianu.

titirasimanigit

tanna takujasa akinisatarijaulautu amisunut kinatuinakunut. tiakani sanaguatisijikalaumat imminutunik, inusimit, ammalu tukunimik, qaujimanatunik qaujimanagitunilu. kinakut ilijilaumangata sanajaviniminik ujaramik, tugani qilalugaup sauninganik uvatinut takujasautilugit.

Hon. Jean Chrétien angajuka inulirijikunut kavamakunu kanatami, (takuninga kanatamiunik inuit sanaguagaginik kamajinik ikajulautuk ukautiluni ammalu aulasijiuluni) pisiatumarialulautuk ikajusasuni ikajurialuni tassuma aqitaulanianingata pigianigani. tanna ammalu ittunisait ikanaijatukutigit – kinaujamut, akilautut, ammalu isumakasialautu – ikajulutik akaungigutaujunik anigutusiluti taimanna akaugigutaulausimagitunik asiagut.

Hon. Mitchell Sharp, titiratiujuk takujasalirijikunut, kavamami kanatami, atanailitisimajuk llunanginut aulakatariasak llangijaulutik tatsuma pinasuvingata pinasuninganu angilivalianingata Ilagijauninganu pikatikaluni asinginik nunanik ammalu Ikanaijatukutigit atuguami ammalu nunait asiani lkajuluni akikatasuni takuninga amisunik Qimiruvinik kanataup silatanitunik takujasanik takujatuviulatunik.

Hon. Donald S. Macdonald angajuka kanutuinak ippigusunimut, kavamamik kanatamik, tanna ikajulautuk qangatasukut ingirajunik takujasaulutik tavungalimak amiarikait nunangata taranu ammalu iuripiup nunanganukatatunik.

Stuart M. Hodgson, angajuka isumata inuit nunangata kavamanganu nunasiamut, titirasimajunut ikajugumaluni. tamakinu kinaujamut ammalu pinasutuit ikauninginut, aksualu pijariakasimama pitsianingit tasumiga aksualu sanaguaraup pigianinganut inuit nunangani nunasiami.

Dr William E. Taylor, Jr angajuka, ilunanginut qimiruvimi uvasiarunitanik atuguami pigiasuni aksualu pijariakasimaju ammalu pijariakamaritu ikajusisimamat taimanna aqitauninga takujasait. tunijaulautugut, imminilutungituk ammalu kanutuinak qaujimaninganut inuit nunangani, ila inikatu qimiruviminik pinasuvisamik, ammalu atuinakakataluni ukluit ilangini, ukllu naamat kamajikaluni ammalu ikajutikalluni takunangat pinasutiminik.

Qujanamipugut aksualu Ikanaijatinik, ammalu amisunik ukataujunik tamaani, takujatukuvini nunani taikani takujasanik takujatuviulatunik, pitakatinagit takua piusatut ammalu Quviangijakatut takujasait sivulipagugutaumat katigutaugajaningitut.

kanatami sanagualirijiit quranamigutikalautut ikajuniminut agilitisigiasak kinaujanik ilagijaugutigilautatinik takujasaliulaniatunut tanna tikitisilautuk angijumik nuasinimik katisisini.

nakusapugut quviasupugut aksualu ikajugumalaumata angajukanik takuninga angilautunik aullatitaulaumata pinasunimut aullasimalutik anaraminik akunialuk.

M. Marcel Evrard uvasiagunitanik akuninitanik qimiruvimiuk parasimi tunisilautuk takujasananik ikajusuni immanut piusaniminut ilagijausuni issumakasiatumut kamajimut ilijaulutik kamagijaulutik taimasainaugituk tunijaulutik taikani nunami.

pijunatuk nitaningipat ammalu pijarialinik pijasanik pijunalaugipat Miss Sharon Van Raalte takujasanut ikajulautuk kaujimalaumat, pinasugasak pijarisiagunagajalaugituk kamalaungipat. Mrs Alma Houston naup qaujimaninganut ammalu quajimautinganut akisimanikalautut qanuiinirilautagit pijariakanirilatanginik qaujigumagaluagata.

Mrs Doris Shadbolt, angajuka vanakuvajaup qimiguavingani, kamajiulautuk aklugitualumit pinasusuni angajukagunimut takunuga takujatuvilirijikunut pitsiaginalautuk imminikigunasuni, tammagisiasuni ukutaminik, ammalu qanuilunirijanga aksualu pitsialautuk. pinasuatumarialuninga takujasalirijiukatausuni: kamajiusuni, James Houston aqisuijik, titiratik aksualu pikatigijaujuk inuit nunangata tititujatiginut, ammalu sunatuinani iliniatisiji George Swinton iliniavijuamit manatupami tititujani iliniavigani, titiratik ammalu kamajiusuni tititujanginik, takua ilaukataujut kaujimanigit ammalu kaujimaningita akisimaningit. takua takujasaiit niruatausutik akitakautut: ammalu Miss Barbara Tyler, angajuka kamajiusuni (ukausilirijiasunilu) sunatuinanik qimirukuvimi takujasakuvimi, atuguami.

GEORGE ELLIOTT
Angajuka
Kanatamiut inuit Sanagualirijinga

Taisumanialuk –
prehistoric Canadian Eskimo art

To give even a brief introduction to prehistoric Canadian Eskimo art one must sketch the still little-known archaeology of Canadian Eskimos. Perhaps that story is the vital, the most meaningful, setting for these objects that voice their eloquence from a long cold silence.

To study Eskimo origins archaeologists must define Eskimo culture, and that is much less easy than it sounds. Usually, the prehistorian considers the Eskimo pattern to entail a distinctive culture adapted to the treeless region – the tundra – and including a mixed hunting economy harvesting land game and fish and marked by a considerable ability in the hunting of sea mammals, such as seals, bearded seals, walrus, and whale. Using such a definition, the earliest known proto-Eskimo are those of the Cape Denbigh Flint complex of northwestern Alaska. This complex dates to about 2000 BC, at which time its people summered on the Bering Strait coast and hunted seal there, perhaps with the use of boats, while other Denbigh people lived in the Alaskan interior depending mainly on caribou. The Denbigh people are known almost solely from their flint tools, scrapers, points, bone-working tools, gouging tools, knife blades, and so on. Among them are some of the most delicately chipped, precisely formed, stone tools in the entire prehistoric world. Denbigh types and styles show enough similarity to those of older Asian sites that most workers believe much of Denbigh origins lie in the Palaeolithic and the Mesolithic of the Far East and in the early Neolithic, say about 4000 BC, of Siberia. Some of the explanations and data on Denbigh origins probably rest in sites that were on the broad Bering land bridge that once joined Siberia and Alaska; that land bridge, however, has been submerged for several millennia by the higher seas resulting from the melting of the great continental ice sheets. Some influence may also have come to the Denbigh heritage from earlier Indian cultures to the south in the North American interior.

Recent Alaskan and Canadian arctic excavations and radiocarbon dates combine to indicate that the Denbigh Flint complex is the classic phase of a series of earlier developmental stages in Alaska and that these stages, as yet undiscovered by pioneering prehistorians, date to between 3500 BC and 2500 BC. It must be from that period and those undiscovered cultures, ancestral to the Denbigh Flint complex, that the earliest Canadian arctic culture and population derived by migration from Alaska.

Whatever their precise origins, Denbigh people, their immediate ancestors, and their direct descendants were well equipped to survive in the Arctic. Their fine environmental adaptation is obvious in the speed with which they successfully spread eastward across arctic Canada to northeast Greenland which they reached before 2000 BC. By the same time that vast, thin drift of population had spread down the west side of Hudson Bay to Churchill and through Baffin Island to the Ungava Peninsula and the Labrador coast.

In Canada this first period of human occupation is called Pre-Dorset, and these east-drifting, Pre-Dorset descendants of an earlier proto-Denbigh people must have been on the central arctic coast of Canada not later than 2500 BC. Their culture stage lasted in Canada until approximately 800 BC, and in southwestern Greenland until about 500 BC. We know rather more of these people than we do about Denbigh for in the permafrost of the Canadian Arctic, far better preservation conditions prevail. Pre-Dorset people lived in small, widely scattered, seasonally nomadic

bands who used skin tents in summer, and small villages of partly under-
ground huts in winter. They used toggling harpoons to hunt seal and
walrus, and bows and arrows for caribou. They also, of course, speared
fish and birds. Their extensive array of chipped flint tools clearly echoes
their proto-Denbigh ancestry, although the stone chipping is not so refined
as that of the classic Denbigh culture. By about 800 BC Pre-Dorset had
evolved into what the archaeologist calls Dorset culture, the distinctive
central and eastern arctic descendant of Pre-Dorset. Although the two are
basically alike, Dorset is recognizably different in many details important
to an archaeologist, if to no one else. Characteristic items include bone
needles, harpoon heads, lances, fish spears, soapstone lamps, and a wide
range of chipped stone tools. Unlike Pre-Dorset, Dorset sites include
ground slate points, and this is an idea that Dorset culture might possibly
have borrowed from prehistoric Indians living in the forest region to the
south.

The oldest scraps of human bones yet found in arctic Canada date to
about 500 BC, and come from Tyara, a Dorset site on the south side of
Hudson Strait. These bones suggest that the Dorset people were physically
Eskimo. Their many sites, the thousands of artifacts collected from them,
their characteristic hunting economy, and the distinctive, small scale,
elegant art reveal their culture to be clearly in the Eskimo pattern.

Some of the Skraelings encountered by Leif Ericson in Vinland were
surely Newfoundland Dorset Eskimo, for Dorset sites are spread widely
from Coronation Gulf in the west to Newfoundland Island and eastern
Greenland in the east. Dorset lasted from about 800 BC to AD 1300 in some
areas, but it began to be crowded off the arctic stage around AD 900 by
a new culture, Thule, then pushing east by migration from northern
Alaska eventually to Greenland and to Labrador. Thule people and Thule
culture derived from a long, developmental sequence of Eskimo cultures
in Alaska, a sequence in part traceable back to the old Denbigh Flint complex of 2000 BC. That prehistoric sequence often incorporated subsequent
influences deriving from Asia.

We do not yet know much about the transition from the Dorset to the
Canadian variant of Thule but some exchange very probably occurred
between the two. In fact, it is quite likely that Thule people learned to
make snow houses from their Dorset predecessors, for it seems a purely
Canadian invention, being absent from the Alaskan variants of Eskimo,
and Thule, culture. Although Dorset and Thule were basically rather
similar in their tundra adaptation, major differences distinguish them.

Presumably Thule people had a more effective arctic adaptation, and this is best seen in their possession of the full range of gear for hunting the great baleen whales, a major food supply never available to the Dorset people who lacked the various techniques, including the umiaks, by which baleen whales were hunted. Indeed, whaling is the most distinctive feature of Thule culture, and artifacts of baleen and whale bone occur abundantly in typical Thule sites. Thule people were classic Eskimo in race, in language, and in culture. They used a complete range of Eskimo items including characteristic fur clothing and boots, kayaks, umiaks, snow houses, weapons, tools, utensils, the shaman's drum, even the typical toys, such as the ajaqaq. They undoubtedly had religious, social, and intellectual systems much like those of the recent Canadian Eskimo. Their first appearance on the historic stage, that is to say, within the time of written records, occurs in the accounts of Martin Frobisher, for when he was shot in the buttocks by an Eskimo arrow at Frobisher Bay, a Thule culture Eskimo launched that arrow.

Thule people were the direct physical and cultural ancestors of the recent and modern Canadian Eskimo including the Caribou Eskimo who turned to the interior west of Hudson Bay. The collapse of Thule whaling explains much of the difference between Thule and recent Eskimo. It seems that in the 18th century whaling was largely abandoned in the Canadian Arctic. A phase of colder climate from AD 1650 to AD 1850, shallower seas, and the diligence over several centuries of European whalers may help to explain the collapse of Thule whaling. With that decrease in their food resources, Thule people had to abandon their large, permanent, winter villages of sturdy houses made of whale bones, sod, and stone slabs. They had then to take up a more nomadic life as they became increasingly dependent on the smaller, more scattered seal and walrus. This subsistence shift demanded a much wider use of the snow house and especially of the snow house village on the sea ice in winter. The other major change from Thule to recent culture, of course, was the arrival of the European explorers, the traders, the missions, the government leading up to such things as school teachers, the DEW line – and tourists.

Turning to the art of the Pre-Dorset, Dorset, and Thule cultures, one must remember that, by their archaeological nature, these examples give only a fragment of the whole art and often only a fragment of the whole artifact.

As yet, almost no art has been reported from the Pre-Dorset culture although incised decoration of bone, antler, or ivory objects is known. Nevertheless, there is possibly an indirect way to glimpse Pre-Dorset art because we know something of Dorset art and because it is now generally agreed, among arctic archaeologists, that Dorset culture evolved from Pre-Dorset culture. This allows the hypothesis that Pre-Dorset and Dorset art must share attributes and concepts, forms and functions in fair degree. If the hypothesis is correct then Pre-Dorset art must be essentially a magico-religious art founded in shamanism and burial rites and an art incorporating amulets, carvings of spirit helpers, small sculptures in the round, human depictions, animal motifs especially the bear, incised designs including crosses and the so-called skeletal motif, and realistic and other styles of expression. It presumably would also be, like Dorset art, small scale, customarily in bone, antler, ivory, and, in lucky cases of preservation, bits of driftwood.

Preserved by the combination of permanently frozen soil and a very low level of bacterial action, Dorset sculptures, the silent echoes of long vanished tribes, of their dead dreams, fears, and strivings, are by far the most lucid and living objects to come into the warming hands of an archaeologist groping through the tundra's millennia. Hardly primitive, it is rather an aboriginal art reflecting a long heritage of development and an art inextricably fused to a religion through which Dorset men knew the unknown. Although it has no direct relation with the art of prehistoric Europe, Dorset art inevitably recalls the European Aurignacian and Magdelanian periods when primitive men persisted in the chill shadows of a vast glacier. Surely these disparate groups of hunters and their families faced the same implacable basic problems with similar intellects and comparable supernatural solutions – men who will seem rather like us in another 20,000 years. The Dorset art shown here provides an evocative survey of this sentient art.

Contrasting with the fine sense of craft and the painstaking finishing of bone, antler, ivory, and stone tools of the Dorset culture, the objects in the subsequent Canadian Thule culture show generally a more utilitarian attitude, for Thule artifacts are seldom so well finished, usually only casually polished, and customarily less neatly shaped. Decoration rarely achieves any significance in Canadian Thule culture and, while art pieces are rare in Dorset culture, they are markedly more rare in Thule sites. Indeed, excavating a Dorset midden one always hopes to uncover a little sculpture, but in a Thule ruin finding an art piece brings not only pleasure but also surprise. Further, no one has yet documented any significant relationship between Dorset and Thule art in arctic Canada. Nor is there any known relationship between the known pieces of Thule art and that culture's shamanism. However, in the rapidly expanding study of Eskimo prehistory, each of the two preceding negative statements might be refuted at any time by new field work.

Excepting their unknown efforts of decorative art in fur, skin, and wood, Canadian Thule culture people expressed their artifactual art in the occasional gracefully formed harpoon head, needle case, or snow goggles, or in bone, antler, or ivory combs, dolls, small bird figures, and, in a few cases, by incised pictographic art.

Recent Eskimo art, influenced by whaler scrimshaw, seldom earns marked regard and that fact makes more remarkable the explosion of contemporary Eskimo art, in stone, ivory, and bone sculptures, and in prints, that began some 22 years ago. To comprehend the process and texture of that phenomenon one should read Charles Martijn's outstanding analysis 'Canadian Eskimo Carvings in Historical Perspective' (*Anthropos*, Vol. LIX, Fribourg, 1965), George Swinton's gracious *Eskimo Sculpture* (McClelland and Stewart, Toronto, 1965) and Robert Williamson's poetic 'The Spirit of Keewatin' (*The Beaver*, Summer issue, Winnipeg, 1965). For a general survey of the art of North American Eskimos one is referred to 'Eskimo Art,' a special Autumn, 1967, issue of *The Beaver* published by the Hudson's Bay Co., Winnipeg.

WILLIAM E. TAYLOR, JR

This is a revision of an article in *Chefs-d'oeuvre des arts indiens et esquimaux du Canada / Masterpieces of Indian and Eskimo art from Canada* by Société des Amis du Musée de l'Homme, Paris, 1969.

Taisumanialuk – l'art préhistorique des Esquimaux du Canada

Il n'est guère possible de parler de l'art préhistorique des Esquimaux du Canada sans donner un aperçu de l'archéologie, encore très peu connue il est vrai, des régions qui l'ont vu naître. C'est, en effet, le contexte le plus significatif, le contexte vital de ces obets qui clament leur éloquence du fond du silence séculaire des glaces.

Pour étudier les origines des Esquimaux, l'archéologue doit commencer par définir la culture esquimaude, ce qui n'est pas aussi facile qu'on pourrait le croire. Pour la plupart des historiens, il s'agit d'une culture particulière adaptée à une terre sans arbres, la toundra, dont l'économie repose sur la chasse et la pêche et les habitants manifestent une aptitude remarquable pour la chasse aux mammifères marins comme le phoque, le phoque barbu, le morse et la baleine. D'après cette définition, les premiers proto-Esquimaux connus sont ceux du complexe du Silex taillé du cap

dans le sud-ouest du Groenland.

Nous connaissons mieux ces peuplades que celles du Denbigh, le permafrost de l'Arctique canadien étant des plus favorables à la conservation de vestiges. Nomades saisonniers, les hommes du Dorset vivaient en petites bandes éparpillées sous des tentes de peaux l'été, dans des petits villages de huttes partiellement souterraines l'hiver. Ils chassaient le phoque et le morse au moyen de harpons à tête mobile et le caribou à l'arc et aux flèches. En outre, ils pêchaient le poisson au dard et chassaient les oiseaux. Leur vaste panoplie d'outils en silex taillé reflète clairement leur origine proto-Denbigh, bien qu'ils ne taillent pas la pierre avec le raffinement propre à la culture classique du Denbigh. Vers 800 av. J-C, le pré-Dorset était devenu, dans l'Arctique central et oriental, ce que les archéologues appellent la culture Dorset. Même si ces deux cultures sont fondamentalement semblables et se rejoignent par de nombreux détails, elles diffèrent sensiblement par de nombreux autres, non moins importants pour l'archéologue. Parmi les éléments caractéristiques, citons les aiguilles d'os, les têtes de harpons, les lances, les dards à poisson, les lampes en stéatite et un vaste choix d'outils en pierre taillée. Contrairement à ceux du pré-Dorset, les sites archéologiques du Dorset renferment aussi des pointes d'ardoise broyée, que la culture Dorset a peut-être empruntées aux Indiens préhistoriques qui vivaient dans les forêts plus au sud.

Les plus anciens restes d'os humains découverts jusqu'à présent dans l'Arctique canadien remontent à l'an 500 environ av. J-C, et proviennent de Tyara, site Dorset situé sur la rive sud du détroit d'Hudson. Ils semblent indiquer que les Dorsétiens étaient physiquement des Esquimaux. Les sites archéologiques et les milliers d'objets ouvrés qu'ils ont laissés, l'importance de la chasse dans leur économie, la grande beauté et la taille très réduite de leurs objets d'art confirment que leur culture appartenait également au type de cultures esquimaudes.

Certains Skraelings que Leif Ericson a rencontrés au Vinland étaient sûrement des Dorsétiens de Terre-Neuve, les sites Dorset étant largement répandus du Golfe du Couronnement, à l'ouest, jusqu'à Terre-Neuve et à l'est du Groenland. La culture Dorset s'est maintenue dans certaines régions environ de 800 av. J-C, à 1300 ap. J-C, mais elle a commencé à être repoussée de la scène arctique vers 900 ap. J-C, par une nouvelle culture, celle de Thulé, qui, du nord de l'Alaska, devait s'étendre jusqu'au Groenland et au Labrador. Le peuple et la culture de Thulé découlent d'une longue séquence évolutive des cultures esquimaudes en Alaska, séquence qu'on peut retracer en partie jusqu'à l'ancien complexe du Silex taillé du cap

Denbigh, dans le nord-ouest de l'Alaska, dont la culture remonte aux environs de l'an 2000 av. J-C, et qui passaient l'été sur la côte du détroit de Béring et y chassaient le phoque (peut être en bateau), tandis que leurs frères de l'intérieur de l'Alaska vivaient principalement de la chasse au caribou. Nous ne connaissons les Denbighiens que par leurs outils de silex, racloirs, pointes, outils à creuser les os, gouges, lames de couteaux, etc., dont certains comptent parmi les plus délicatement taillés, les plus parfaitement formés de l'époque préhistorique. Les modèles et les styles du Denbigh présentent une telle ressemblance avec ceux des anciens sites archéologiques de l'Asie que la plupart des chercheurs associent les origines du Denbigh au paléolithique et au mésolithique de l'Extrême-Orient et au néolithique, (v. 4000 av. J-C) sibérien. Le large pont naturel de Béring qui reliait autrefois la Sibérie à l'Alaska recèle probablement des explications et des données sur les origines de la culture du complexe du Silex taillé du cap Denbigh, mais il est englouti depuis plusieurs millénaires par suite de la fonte des calottes glaciaires qui a entraîné une élévation du niveau des océans. Le patrimoine du Denbigh peut aussi s'être enrichi de l'apport des cultures indiennes déjà installées dans le nord de l'Amérique.

De récentes excavations en Alaska et dans l'Arctique canadien et la datation au carbone 14 s'accordent pour indiquer que le complexe du Silex taillé du cap Denbigh constitue la période classique, l'aboutissement d'une série d'étapes évolutives que les pionniers de l'étude de la préhistoire n'ont pas encore découvertes et qui se situeraient entre 3500 et 2500 av. J-C. Les migrations aidant, ces cultures inconnues de l'Alaska, ancêtres du complexe du Silex taillé du Denbigh, auraient donné naissance à la première culture et au premier peuple arctiques du Canada.

Quelle que soit son origine précise, le peuple du Denbigh, ses ancêtres immédiats et ses descendants étaient équipés pour survivre dans l'Arctique. Ils ont prouvé leur étonnante faculté d'adaptation à leur environnement par la rapidité avec laquelle ils se sont dispersés à travers l'Arctique canadien jusqu'à la côte nord-ouest du Groenland qu'ils ont atteinte avant l'an 2000 av. J-C, tout en poussant à l'ouest de la baie d'Hudson jusqu'à Churchill et, à travers l'île de Baffin, jusqu'à la péninsule de l'Ungave et la côte du Labrador.

Au Canada, cette première période d'occupation humaine a reçu l'appellation de pré-Dorset et les descendants pré-Dorsétiens d'une peuplade du proto-Denbigh ont dû atteindre, dans leur poussée vers l'est, la côte de l'Arctique central du Canada avant l'an 2500 av. J-C. Leur culture devait durer au Canada jusqu'aux environs de 800 av. J-C, et trois siècles encore

Denbigh de l'an 2000 av. J-C, et dans laquelle on reconnaît certaines influences asiatiques ultérieures.

Nous n'avons pas encore beaucoup de données sur la transition entre le Dorset et la variante canadienne de la culture Thulé mais il y a très probablement eu des échanges entre les deux cultures. En fait, le peuple Thulé a vraisemblablement appris de son prédécesseur dorsétien l'art de fabriquer des maisons de neige puisqu'il semble s'agir d'une invention strictement canadienne, qu'on ne retrouve pas chez les autres peuplades esquimaudes de Thulé qui habitaient l'Alaska. Bien que les Dorsétiens et le peuple Thulé se rejoignent par leur adaptation à la vie dans l'Arctique, d'importantes différences les séparent. Il est probable que le peuple Thulé s'est adapté à l'Arctique de façon plus efficace. C'est ainsi qu'il possède des accessoires, tel l'umiak, qui lui permettent de chasser la grande baleine, source abondante de nourriture à laquelle les Dorsétiens n'avaient pas accès justement parce qu'ils ne connaissaient pas ces techniques. La chasse à la baleine est caractéristique de la culture Thulé et on retrouve, dans les sites Thulé, des artefacts de fanons et d'os de baleine en abondance. Le peuple Thulé était de race, de langue et de culture esquimaudes classiques. Il disposait de toute la gamme d'objets esquimaux caractéristiques, comme les vêtements et les bottes de fourrure, les kayaks, les umiaks, les maisons de neige, les armes, les outils, les ustensiles, le tambour du chaman et même les jouets tels l'ajaqaq. Ses croyances religieuses, son ordre social et sa façon de penser étaient très proches de ceux des cultures esquimaudes modernes. C'est dans les récits de voyage de Martin Frobisher qu'une référence y est faite pour la première fois dans un document écrit: la flèche esquimaude qui a blessé l'explorateur à l'arrière-train dans la baie de Frobisher avait été lancée par un Esquimau de culture Thulé.

Le peuple Thulé est l'ancêtre physique et culturel en ligne droite des Esquimaux modernes, y compris ceux du Caribou, qui se sont dirigés vers l'intérieur des terres, à l'ouest de la baie d'Hudson. L'effondrement de la chasse à la baleine explique en grande partie les différences existant entre la culture Thulé et celle des Esquimaux d'aujourd'hui. C'est au dix-huitième siècle que les Thulé semblent avoir abandonné ce mode de chasse dans l'Arctique canadien. Parmi les facteurs qui ont contribué à précipiter ce délaissement, citons la vague de froid qui a sévi de 1650 à 1850, la baisse du niveau des mers et la diligence des baleiniers européens au cours de ces derniers siècles. Face à cette diminution brutale de leurs réserves de vivres, le peuple Thulé s'est vu contraint de quitter les grands villages permanents d'hiver et leurs solides maisons en os de baleines, tourbe et dalles de pierre pour adopter un mode de vie nomade à la poursuite des phoques et des morses. D'où la popularité des maisons de neige et l'apparition des campements de neige sur la glace maritime en hiver. L'autre facteur d'importance à l'origine du passage de la culture Thulé à la culture esquimaude moderne est évidemment l'arrivée des explorateurs, des commerçants, des missionnaires et gouvernements européens, puis des maîtres d'école, du réseau avancé de pré-alerte (DEW) et…des touristes.

Avant d'aborder la question de l'art dans les cultures pré-Dorset, Dorset et Thulé, il faut se rappeler que, de par leur nature archéologique, les objets qui nous sont parvenus ne représentent qu'un fragment de cet art, souvent même un fragment d'une seule oeuvre.

Jusqu'à présent, on n'a découvert aucune oeuvre d'art provenant de la culture pré-Dorset, dont on connaît toutefois des objets décoratifs d'os, de corne et d'ivoire gravés. Il est néanmoins possible d'avoir un aperçu de l'art pré-dorsétien à travers l'art dorsétien puisque les archéologues sont généralement d'accord quant à l'origine pré-dorsétienne de la culture Dorset. Forts de cette caution scientifique, nous pouvons donc formuler l'hypothèse que les arts du pré-Dorset et du Dorset partagent sensiblement les mêmes attributs et les mêmes concepts, les mêmes formes et les mêmes fonctions. Si notre hypothèse est exacte, l'art pré-dorsétien est essentiellement un art magico-religieux fondé sur le chamanisme et les rites funéraires et qui prend la forme d'amulettes, de sculptures d'esprits bénéfiques, d'autres petites sculptures de ronde-bosse, de formes humaines, de motifs d'animaux représentant souvent l'ours, d'images gravées, dont des croix et le motif dit du squelette, traités de manière réaliste ou non. Comme celles du Dorset, ces oeuvres seraient probablement de petite taille, habituellement en os, en corne, en ivoire et en bois flotté.

Conservées grâce à l'heureuse combinaison d'un sol gelé en permanence et d'un niveau très bas d'activité bactérienne, les sculptures dorsétiennes, échos silencieux des tribus ensevelies dans la nuit des temps, de leurs rêves, de leurs craintes et de leurs luttes, sont de loin les objets les plus lucides et les plus vivants qui puissent tomber entre les mains avides d'un archéologue explorant les millénaires de la toundra. L'on ne peut guère qualifier de 'primitif' cet art aborigène qui reflète une longue évolution culturelle, art inextricablement fusionné à une religion qui permettait aux hommes du Dorset de connaître l'inconnu. Bien qu'il n'ait aucun lien direct avec l'art préhistorique européen, il rappelle inévitablement les époques européennes de l'aurignacien et du magdalénien, époques où les hommes s'entêtaient à survivre à l'ombre d'un vaste glacier. Ces groupes disparates de chasseurs et leurs familles affrontaient sûrement les mêmes problèmes fondamentaux implacables, ils possédaient une intelligence semblable et des solutions surnaturelles comparables ... et, dans 20,000 ans, on nous confondra avec eux. Les exemples d'art dorsétien que nous exposons offrent un aperçu évocateur de cet art sensible.

Contrastant avec l'art raffiné et la finition méticuleuse des outils d'os, de corne, d'ivoire et de pierre de la culture du Dorset, les objets de la culture Thulé démontrent une attitude plus utilitaire de la part des artistes qui les ont créés. Leur finition est rarement aussi soignée, ils sont polis d'une façon quelconque et leurs formes sont moins bien définies. La décoration n'y a guère d'importance et les objets d'art, déjà rares dans la culture dorsétienne, le sont encore davantage dans celle de Thulé. Tandis qu'il est permis, en fouillant des débris du Dorset, d'espérer toujours qu'on tombera sur une petite sculpture, la découverte d'un objet d'art dans une ruine du Thulé est une surprise autant qu'une joie. En outre, personne n'a pu à ce jour démontrer une relation significative entre les arts du Dorset et de la culture Thulé dans l'Arctique canadien. Il n'y a pas non plus de relation connue entre les objets d'art de Thulé et le chamanisme de cette culture. Réciproquement, étant donné les progrès des études de la préhistoire esquimaude, de nouveaux travaux d'exploration peuvent à n'importe quel moment venir réfuter les deux énoncés ci-dessus.

Un des aspects inexplicables de l'art dorsétien, c'est qu'il semble possible de découvrir une explication de sa signification dans la littérature du début du vingtième siècle qui traite du chamanisme, des symboles et des croyances des Esquimaux modernes du centre du Canada et des Esquimaux du Groenland. Ce système de croyances provient en grande partie de la culture Thulé et suggère donc l'existence, au sein de celle-ci, de croyances qui expliqueraient certains éléments de l'art du Dorset, malgré l'absence générale déjà notée de preuves indiquant une forte continuité culturelle entre l'art dorsétien et le système de croyances qu'il suggère d'une part, et, d'autre part, l'art et les croyances de la culture Ipiutak qui existait dans le nord-ouest de l'Alaska vers l'an 300 de notre ère. Bien que rien ne laisse supposer l'existence d'une relation directe entre les cultures du Dorset et d'Ipiutak, il est possible que les ressemblances entre elles proviennent du patrimoine commun légué par le complexe du Silex taillé du cap Denbigh.

A l'exception de tentatives hypothétiques d'art décoratif sur les fourrures, les peaux et le bois, l'art artisanal de la culture Thulé prend la forme d'objets aux contours gracieux, têtes de harpon, coffres à aiguilles ou lunettes à neige, de peignes d'os, de corne ou d'ivoire, de poupées, de petites figurines d'oiseaux ou, parfois, de dessins gravés.

L'art esquimau moderne, influencé par les petits objets de fantaisie fabriqués par les équipages de baleiniers, mérite rarement une attention particulière, ce qui met encore davantage en relief l'explosion de l'art esquimau contemporain, sculptures de pierre, d'ivoire et d'os et estampes, dont le début date d'il y a environ 22 ans. Pour comprendre l'essence de ce phénomène, il faut lire la remarquable analyse de Charles Martijn intitulée 'Canadian Eskimo Carvings in Historical Perspective' (Anthropos, Vol. LIX, Fribourg, 1965), le charmant ouvrage de George Swinton, Eskimo Sculpture (McClelland and Stewart, Toronto, 1965) et le poétique 'The Spirit of Keewatin' de Robert Williamson (The Beaver, numéro d'été, Winnipeg, 1965). On trouvera aussi une étude générale de l'art des Esquimaux de l'Amérique du Nord dans 'Eskimo Art' numéro spécial d'automne 1967 de la revue The Beaver, publiée par la Compagnie de la Baie d'Hudson, à Winnipeg.

WILLIAM E. TAYLOR JR

Ceci est une révision d'un article dans Chefs-d'oeuvre des arts indiens et esquimaux du Canada / Masterpieces of Indian and Eskimo art from Canada par la Société des Amis du Musée de l'Homme, Paris, 1969.

Contemporary
Canadian Eskimo sculpture

Like most other contemporary art forms and movements, Canadian Eskimo sculpture is derived from many traditions. Yet its most important
characteristic is innovation rather than derivation or traditionalism.

When the contemporary phase had its beginnings between 1948 and
1952, attempts were made in many quarters to give respectability to the
new movement by linking it with the past. However, these well-intended
attempts backfired and their conspicuous promotion generated art-histori-
cal and anthropological suspicions and prejudgments against the new art.
These are only gradually being broken down by the slow process of sorting
out the immense production of carvings that has taken place in the last
twenty years and by the perceptible emergence of several individual
artists of stature. Also, the former, largely public-relations oriented litera-
ture about the new art form has become obsolete and is, fortunately, being

replaced by more critical and knowledgeable studies. And in addition to (and partially as a result of) all these developments, an ever increasing interest in collecting contemporary Eskimo art, both privately and publicly, has become noticeable.

Three basic misconceptions about the new art form need to be resolved. First, it is undoubtedly wrong to speak of 'Eskimo art' (or of 'Eskimo sculpture') as if this were one single, unified, ethnic art form when, in fact, regional, local, and highly individual style characteristics are so dominant. Second, contemporary Eskimo life is entirely different from what it used to be in the distant past, or even ten years ago; today's Eskimos are no longer nomads but live in an urbanized society oriented toward white technology. Third, sculpture is only one of several new art forms which have found roots in the contemporary Arctic: the other most prominent are printmaking (stone cuts, engravings, stencil, and silk-screen prints), drawing, occasionally painting, and ceramics (at Rankin Inlet).

To people who know something about Eskimo art past and present, it must sound strange to hear their sculpture being called a 'new' art form. Yet considering the nature and the essential motivation of the recent carving, it actually is. In the 150 years before 1948/49 – and in many areas much more recently – carving was mostly functional, decorative, and, if figurative, casual or recreational, but certainly not an art activity in our sense of the word. That is to say, Eskimo people carved to make tools, utensils, weapons, toys, whittles, and, occasionally, souvenirs – replicas – for visiting whites. And interestingly enough, as in so many other non-literate cultures, there is no Eskimo word for art. Yet the idea of image-making has existed in the Arctic for at least 2800 years.

Today the word that is being used for carving is *sananguaq* or *sana-nguagaq*[1] which has a significant etymological derivation: *sana* refers to 'making' and *nguaq* to the idea of 'model, imitation, or likeness.' In Alaska, by the way, *nguaq* refers to 'play pretending' and in Greenland it signifies 'little' in a sense of a diminutive. Indeed there are several related words which use the suffix *nguaq* to express the diminutive-likeness-imitation-model-play connotation. They are *inunguaq* – doll, 'a little man-likeness'; *pinguaq* – toy, 'a little pretend-toying'; and *atjinguaq*, which means 'a likeness like a replica' and is hence used as an Eskimo word for photograph. The carving-*sananguaq* idea refers then to a likeness that is made or fabricated, that is, handicrafted. When the great Cape Dorset artist Kenojuak was once asked what the word for art is, she answered: 'There is no word for art,' *sananguatavut* – 'we say it is from the real to the

37

unreal.' This is not too happy a translation, as fascinating as it may sound. For *sananguatavut* deals not so much with the idea of the real and unreal as with the idea of having succeeded in making a likeness: 'we have taken and made it a likeness' – 'a little likeness we have achieved by making it.' The imitation is not unreal but actually a little replica – 'a little likeness-reality that we have achieved.'

This point needs much emphasis because it leads to an understanding of the whole nature of contemporary Eskimo art which is essentially the achievement of making likenesses – real or imagined – which have their own diminutive reality rather than beauty. Indeed, not unsimilar to our own contemporary concepts! A carving is then an object that is well made rather than beautiful and this is the essential criterion for judgment: the success of the artist in having worked the stone well, in having reacted sensitively and intelligently to the material from which the carving is made, and in capturing the imitation – the likeness. The Eskimo aesthetic is clearly contained in the word *sananguaq*: the emphasis on making and the achieving of likeness, that is, its own reality. Ultimately, since the Eskimo language has no equivalent to 'beauty,' *sananguaq* has now acquired aesthetic connotations, successful achievement implying beauty.[2]

It is with regard to this idea that contemporary art deviates most pronouncedly from the work of the distant past. And it is this deviation (which also includes the unfortunate but readily understandable dearth of magico-religious art) that has sparked most of the controversy surrounding the new art. In the prehistoric Dorset and Thule cultures, art styles were highly collective in terms of both form and content. So much so, in fact, that the proverbial homogeneity of the Eskimo has derived from the superficial acceptance of these resemblances as a typical Eskimo trait.

After the gradual disappearance of the Thule culture in the seventeenth and eighteenth centuries, there occurred a gradual decay of art styles. They were replaced by the predominantly functional, decorative, and casual carvings which lasted until the 'contemporary' post-World War II period. During that transitional phase – apart from the magical amulet carvings (and a large percentage of the amulets were simply 'natural' objects rather than carvings) – art became largely secularized, just as another important aspect of the Eskimo spiritual life had lost much of its sacred content. Hunting, on which all Eskimo life depended in a very direct and personal way, had been a spiritual activity in which the hunter and the hunted had close mystical relationships. But with the coming of the whalers and traders – who were eager to harvest the rich fur bounty of the land, particularly the Arctic fox which of all the animals had the lowest esteem in the mind of the Eskimo hunter – fur trapping was initiated and with it the commercialization and secularization of the hunt, and, because the hunt was the central activity of Eskimo existence, the gradual secularization of Eskimo life.[3]

Concurrently with this development, the Eskimo discovered the potential of carvings as convenient trading objects and there developed quite spontaneously a carving activity whose major, if not sole, purpose was trade and therefore secondary gratification of one's needs. Add to these changes all the other initial aspects of acculturation which came into being as the result of the increasing contacts with the whites (the *kablunait* – the people with the heavy eyebrows), and it is only natural that the character of the art should change under the new circumstances.

It is important to note that this is not a value judgment. While it is feasible to speak of a 'decay of art styles' in the sense of the breakdown of long-standing traditions of collective form (i.e., style), one must not forget that with this breakdown, carving became a much more general activity without a collective style, involving a great many more practitioners, even though they may not be called artists in a formal sense. In fact, it is my firm belief that the large scale carving activities of the nineteenth century established the myth of the universal Eskimo artist because of the very wide practice of carving decorative and casual objects beyond the general functional carving activities.

Dr Charles Martijn and I have described this on several occasions and there is no need to do so again.[4] One should emphasize, however, that these activities are separate from prehistoric traditions and from the contemporary carvings which were so successfully initiated by James A. Houston in 1948/49. Also, one should emphasize that the present activities, though different in scope and quality, have a tradition, however informal, in the non-functional and vicarious aspects of the carvings of the nineteenth century.

One must also add that, although it seriously threatens every aspect of Eskimo cultural and spiritual survival, the entire process of acculturation is a condition of life that has provided means for physical survival which was always first priority for every Eskimo. Now that these conditions have been secured, ethnic and spiritual self-affirmation is gradually emerging as a new priority. And already the young Eskimo turks can be heard rumbling in the background.

Finally, with regard to the transitional carving phase of the nineteenth century and the first half of the twentieth – which frequently is designated as the Historic Period in contrast to the Prehistoric Period (Dorset and Thule) and the Contemporary Period – one must also emphasize some distinctive characteristics of the indigenous pieces and the trade art objects. For they too form an important link between the Historical and the Contemporary traditions.

In the indigenous pieces the emphasis is on function and adequacy rather than aesthetic excellence. In the trade art objects the emphasis is on pleasantness, on being diminutive and exquisitely executed representations of human activities and animal life of the entire Eskimo environment, including replicas of trade objects imported by the *kablunait*. Indigenous art objects of that period often were made crudely[5] and left unfinished, trade art was more highly accomplished. Indigenous objects had a warm and unpretentious aesthetic, an aesthetic of guilelessness – folk art rather than primitive art. Even trade art, though more highly finished and often overly playful, still retained a strong flavour of folk art in spite of its conspicuous 'commercial' aspects.

It was the purely environmental content of all historical Eskimo art that gave it its folk art character. By folk art I mean an art form that is environmentally conditioned, that is, it is related to ideas which arise from folklore or from direct experience of the environment rather than from the more sophisticated aesthetic theories and complex allegoric ideas of so-called 'higher or fine art' forms, which usually have discarded or refined their origins and roots in folk art.

The ambivalent indigenous and trade art aspects on the one hand, and the folk art character on the other, provide an unheralded link between the art of today and the art of the nineteenth century. Today, of course, the rapid rate of acculturation and the extraordinarily far-reaching activities of the international art market have brought about an intensive and more complex development.

The speed and intensity of acculturation of the post-World War II period further polarized the differences between the crude indigenous and the more sophisticated trade carvings. Also, there gradually emerged refinements of the now polarized forms by individual artists – such as Johnnie Inukpuk, Kavik, Latcholassie, Pangnark, Pauta, Charlie Seeguapik, Tasseor, and Tiktak, to name just a few – and more recently an increasing number of fantasy and mythological carvings with strong grotesque and surrealistic aspects of form have appeared. These latter developments occurred independently in Cape Dorset during the early sixties (Aggiak, Audla, Axangayuk, Kiawak, Oshooweetook, and Saggiak), in Povungnituk during the mid-sixties (Davideealuk and Eli Salualuk), and in many other settlements more recently. In fact, it has become possible to observe definite patterns of growth in the various areas with sequences that vary with changing circumstances of exposure and economic development.

Essentially, the sequence begins with the 'crude' stage (which often is mistakenly called 'primitive') followed by refinements that lead into two areas – naturalism and formalization. At that point, unless there is sympathetic evaluation, management, or guidance, a great many art programmes or projects collapse because of exploitation of their own success and end in clichés and repetition. On the other hand, in the more vital localities, individual artists are conspicuously emerging. These artists provide new insights and growth patterns and, generally speaking, are at least partially responsible for the healthy progress in their localities.

One must add, however, that at this stage of development the presence of knowledgeable and sympathetic whites as project officers, traders, or residents has considerable bearing on the success of projects or the development of individual artists. This factor more than any other causes the contemporary activities to differ so considerably from those of the Historic phase, when everyone was left on his own and developments depended on the gradual discovery by the carvers of what the visiting whalers, explorers, or traders liked best. But today, when carving has become almost exclusively an art-for-sale activity, and with prices based on the individual tastes of resident traders or project officers, the contemporary carvers have become very much dependent on those whites who reside more or less permanently in the settlements. Artists at, say, Baker Lake, Cape Dorset, Eskimo Point, Lake Harbour, Port Harrison, Povungnituk, Rankin Inlet, and Repulse Bay have always benefited from the presence of white residents who could give the kind of intelligent and sympathetic leadership that guides but does not control, that encourages but does not direct, and that inspires but does not dictate. Great achievements were thus accomplished in those communities, and now there also has arisen an awareness in the Eskimo artists of the need and their capacity to conduct their own affairs.

Finally, one should mention that in some communities there live a good many artists who can produce well when they produce little, or others who have only a few years of excellent production and then suddenly stop. They are not unlike many artists in the Western world, and to expect a steady stream of great art from an entire group of people is unreasonable and overly naïve. But because of the myth of the 'great-universal-primitive-Eskimo-artist' too much is expected too often.

Also, at the very moment when their spiritual and cultural existence is threatened with extinction, the Eskimo artists are asked to produce in an idiom that expresses and affirms a way of life and a response to their environment which obviously is anachronistic. The miracle is that, instead of failing completely, they often succeed and are able to give us an idea of past Eskimo life. But their art is very much like a swan song, or, even more frighteningly (or perhaps more beautifully), the artists are, like Kierkegaard's poet, unhappy men who in their hearts 'harbor a deep anguish, but whose lips are so fashioned that the moans and cries which pass over them are transformed into ravishing music . . .'

For, undoubtedly, this very quality of the new art, made by people singing of what they no longer are, contains a dual element of tragedy and irony: at its worst it reflects an actual stage of ethnic agony and death, at its best it speaks in a greater degree of what was than of what is.

Yet in addition to the swan song there exists a new idea: the new forms, the emergence of the individuality of artists, the techniques which include economic structures as well as new media, and – most of all – the convincing works that are different from the past, entailing the seeds and growth-hopes for a future that is based on a new environment. The new carvings are becoming a new reality.

As far as spellings of Eskimo names are concerned, it is unfortunately almost impossible to arrive at a consensus. What has therefore been attempted is to use a spelling system that is descriptive of the sounds of the names and that was acceptable to the artists. Hence our spellings were produced in consultation with the artists and in accordance with established practices. It may be assumed, where full names are given, that the Eskimo name is the one commonly used.

In this catalogue the description of materials used is confined to simple terms such as, stone, bone, ivory, etc. This was done to avoid technical confusions which highly specific geological and biological terms might have introduced. Such terms would be more exact, but, usually, they are only more relevant to scientists and not to art viewers.

GEORGE SWINTON

NOTES

1 Pronounced *sha-na-ngu-ak* and *sha-na-ngu-a'-ngak*.

2 These linguistic subtleties have been thoroughly discussed with Professor R. G. Williamson and Professor T. C. Correll.

3 Cf. Robert G. Williamson, 'The Canadian Arctic: Sociocultural Change,' *Arch Environ Health*, 17 (Oct. 1968), 484–91.

4 Cf. Charles A. Martijn, 'Canadian Eskimo Carving in Historical Perspective' *Antleropos*, LIX (1965), 546–96. Charles A. Martijn, 'A Retrospective Glance' *The Beaver*, 298 (Autumn, 1967), 4–19. George Swinton, *Eskimo Sculpture – Sculpture Esquimaude* (McClelland & Stewart, 1965).

5 One should perhaps explain that 'crude' and 'primitive' are not value judgments when used in the context of art. 'Primitive' refers to societies that have not become acculturated and often refers to art that is highly complex, sophisticated, and carefully executed (like NW coast Indian art, to name just one). 'Crude' on the other hand refers to a lack of sophistication and refinement of technique, both qualities that do not necessarily interfere with the content of the work but often enhance it. It implies a quality that is often disarming and pure in its directness and lack of technical gimmickry. In terms of public acceptance crude art has always been down-graded and has therefore led to the more 'acceptable' trade art of the nineteenth century and the tourist art of the twentieth.

A large part of the contemporary production is trade-tourist-souvenir art, which is not astonishing under present acculturation conditions. What is astounding is the large quantity of good art that comes directly from, and exists in spite of, the souvenir production. But that is not really different from our own practices where the cliché outweighs the creative in much larger proportions.

La sculpture contemporaire chez les Esquimaux du Canada

A l'instar des autres mouvements et formes d'art contemporains, la sculpture esquimaude du Canada découle de plusieurs traditions. Ce qui la caractérise davantage, toutefois, ce n'est ni le traditionalisme ni la tendance à emprunter, mais bien l'innovation.

Au début de la période contemporaine, entre 1948 et 1952, on a tenté dans plusieurs milieux de conférer au nouveau mouvement une certaine respectabilité en le reliant au passé. Ces tentatives, sans doute bien intentionnées, ont mal servi le nouvel art en provoquant, par une publicité tapageuse, des soupçons et des préjugés chez les historiens de l'art et les anthropologues. Néanmoins, grâce à l'apparition de quelques artistes de taille et au fur et à mesure du lent triage qu'a subi l'abondante production de sculptures des vingt dernières années, ces soupçons et ces préjugés s'estompent. De plus, la littérature publicitaire et vulgarisante ayant trait au nouvel art maintenant démodé, a été remplacée par des études plus critiques et mieux informées. Ce sont, du reste, tous ces facteurs qui expliquent, en partie, l'intérêt croissant manifesté pour la mise sur pied de collections, tant particulières que publiques, d'art esquimau contemporain.

Le nouvel art fait l'objet de trois conceptions erronées, qu'il importe de dissiper. D'abord, il est faux de parler d' 'art esquimau' (ou de 'sculpture esquimaude') comme s'il n'y avait qu'une seule forme d'art ethnique, unifiée, monolithique, alors qu'effectivement les caractéristiques régionales et locales, ainsi que le style hautement individuel des artistes, jouent un si grand rôle. Ensuite, la vie de l'Esquimau contemporain est très différente de ce qu'elle était jadis ou même il y a à peine dix ans: les Esquimaux d'aujourd'hui ne sont plus nomades, vivant au contraire dans une société urbanisée, orientée vers la technologie des Blancs. Enfin, la sculpture n'est qu'une des nombreuses nouvelles formes d'art qui ont pris naissance dans l'Arctique: l'estampe (lithographie, gravure, estampe au pochoir et sérigraphie), le dessin, la céramique (à Rankin Inlet) et parfois la peinture.

Ceux qui connaissent l'art esquimau d'hier et d'aujourd'hui trouvent sans doute étrange qu'on considère cette sculpture comme une nouvelle forme d'art. Et c'est pourtant le cas si l'on envisage la nature de la sculpture actuelle et la motivation qui en est à la base. Durant les 150 années qui ont précédé 1948 et plus récemment dans plusieurs régions, la sculpture était surtout fonctionnelle, décorative; ce n'est qu'occasionnellement et en guise de divertissement qu'elle est devenue figurative; elle n'était certainement pas une activité artistique au sens habituel de cette expression. C'est donc dire que le peuple esquimau sculptait pour fabriquer des outils, des ustensiles, des armes, des jouets et parfois des souvenirs pour les visiteurs blancs. Et chose assez intéressante, il n'existe pas de mot en esquimau pour désigner l'art, comme c'est d'ailleurs le cas dans beaucoup d'autres cultures de tradition orale. Et pourtant, l'idée de faire des images a cours dans l'Arctique depuis au moins 2,800 ans.

Aujourd'hui, le mot que l'on emploie pour désigner l'action de sculpter est sananguaq ou sananguagaq[1] qui possède une étymologie significative: sana veut dire 'faire' et nguaq se rapporte au concept de 'modèle, imitation, ressemblance'. En Alaska, nguaq signifie 'jouer en faisant semblant' et au Groenland, il signifie 'petit' dans un sens diminutif. Il existe plusieurs mots apparentés qui ajoutent le suffixe nguaq pour exprimer les connotations de diminutif, de ressemblance, d'imitation, de modèle, de jeu: inunguaq (poupée) – 'une ressemblance de petit homme'; pinguaq *(jouet) – 'un petit objet pour jouer à faire semblant'; atjinguaq (ressemblance sous forme de copie ou de réplique) que les Esquimaux emploient pour désigner une photographie. Le concept de 'sculpture-sananguaq' se rapporte donc à une ressemblance qui est faite, fabriquée ou façonnée. Lorsqu'on a demandé à la grande artiste Kenojuak, de Cape Dorset, quel était le mot pour désigner l'art, elle a répondu: 'Il n'y a pas de mot pour désigner l'art – sananguatavut – nous disons que c'est du réel à l'irréel. Pour fascinante qu'elle soit, cette traduction n'est pas tout à fait juste, car sananguatvut rend moins les notions de réel et d'irréel que l'idée d'avoir réussi à faire une ressemblance: 'nous avons fait une ressemblance' – 'une petite ressemblance que nous avons produite en la fabriquant'. L'imitation n'est pas irréelle, puisqu'elle est une petite reproduction, 'une petite réalité que nous avons faite'.*

Il faut insister beaucoup sur cette question, car elle conduit à une compréhension de l'essence même de l'art esquimau contemporain, qui est avant tout la fabrication de ressemblances, vraies ou imaginaires, ayant leur propre réalité diminutive plutôt qu'une certaine beauté plastique. Voilà qui ne diffère pas tellement de nos conceptions contemporaines! Une sculpture est donc un objet bien fait, plutôt qu'un bel objet, et c'est là le critère essentiel d'appréciation: la réussite de l'artiste consiste à bien travailler la pierre, à réagir d'une façon sensible et intelligente devant la matière dont il a tiré sa sculpture, à saisir l'imitation, la ressemblance. L'esthétique esquimaude est nettement comprise dans le mot sananguaq: l'insistance sur la fabrication et sur la réalisation de la ressemblance, c'est-à-dire de la réalité même de cette ressemblance. La langue esquimaude ne disposant pas d'un mot pour exprimer la beauté, sananguaq a par la suite acquis des connotations esthétiques et se réfère à une fabrication réussie possédant une certaine beauté.[2]

Voilà en quoi l'art contemporain se distingue nettement de celui d'antan. Et c'est cette différence qui a provoqué le gros de la controverse entourant le nouvel art et qui explique également la pauvreté déplorable, mais facilement compréhensible, de l'art magico-religieux. Dans les cultures préhistoriques de Dorset et de Thulé, le style artistique était collectif, du double point de vue de la forme et du contenu; l'homogénéité proverbiale des Esquimaux tient à une constatation superficielle de cette uniformité de style artistique, prise pour un trait typique et général de l'Esquimau.

Depuis la disparition graduelle de la culture de Thulé aux dix-septième et dix-huitième siècles, il s'est produit une décadence progressive des styles artistiques, remplacés par des sculptures occasionnelles, surtout fonctionnelles et décoratives. Exception faite des amulettes sculptées (dont une forte proportion était tout simplement des objets naturels, et non des sculptures), l'art a perdu beaucoup de son caractère sacré au cours de la période de transition qui a duré jusqu'à l'après-guerre, phéno-mène qui s'était déjà produit pour un autre aspect important de la vie de l'Esquimau. En effet, la chasse, dont dépendait directement et d'une manière très personnelle toute la vie esquimaude, avait été une activité spirituelle dans laquelle le chasseur et le chassé entretenaient des relations mystiques intimes. De grands changements ont eu lieu lorsque sont arrivés les chasseurs de baleines et les commerçants désireux de s'approprier les grandes ressources de fourrure, dont celle du renard arctique, la moins recherchée du chasseur esquimau. L'avènement du piégeage des animaux à fourrure a entraîné la sécularisation et la commercialisation de la chasse, principle activité de la vie esquimaude; celle-ci n'a donc pas tardé à se séculariser également.[3]

En même temps, les Esquimaux ont découvert l'utilité des sculptures comme objets d'échange et tout spontanément les activités artistiques ont pris de l'ampleur, leur but principal, sinon unique, étant sans doute le commerce et, accessoirement, la satisfaction des besoins personnels. A tous ces changements s'ajoutent, bien sûr, les caractéristiques initiales de l'acculturation qui s'est produite à la suite des contacts de plus en plus nombreux avec les Blancs (les Kablunait – les hommes aux sourcils épais).

Dans de telles circonstances, il est donc tout à fait naturel que les formes d'art se soient modifiées.

Il ne faut pas voir ici un jugement de valeur. Même si l'on peut parler d'une décadence des styles artistiques dans le sens d'un effondrement des traditions séculaires de formes d'art collectives, on ne doit pas oublier que la sculpture est devenue, du même coup, une activité beaucoup plus généralisée, sans style collectif, exercée par plus de praticiens, même si ces derniers ne sont pas tous des artistes au sens strict. En fait, je crois fermement que si la sculpture pratiquée à une très grande échelle au dix-neuvième siècle a engendré le mythe de l'artiste esquimau universel, c'est à cause de la pratique très répandue de sculpter des objets décoratifs s'ajoutant aux objets strictement fonctionnels.

M. Charles Martijn et moi-même avons maintes fois décrit ces acti-vités; il n'y a donc pas lieu de recommencer.[4] Il faut toutefois souligner qu'elles se distinguent des traditions préhistoriques et des sculptures con-temporaines que M. James A. Houston a lancées avec tant de succès en 1948. Autre fait à souligner: même si les activités actuelles ont une ampleur et une qualité différentes, elles s'inspirent d'une tradition qui, si peu formelle soit-elle, participe du caractère non-fonctionnel des sculptures du dix-neuvième siècle.

Bien qu'elle menace la survivance culturelle et spirituelle des Esquimaux, l'acculturation est une condition qui leur a fourni les moyens d'assurer leur survivance physique, celle-ci ayant été de tout temps leur préoccupation première, aujourd'hui supplantée peu à peu par la survivance ethnique et spirituelle. Et l'on entend déjà les revendications parfois arrogantes des jeunes Esquimaux.

En ce qui concerne la période de transition du dix-neuvième siècle et de la première moitié du vingtième siècle, qu'on appelle souvent la Période historique, par opposition à la Période préhistorique (Dorset et Thulé) et à la Période contemporaine, il faut souligner certains traits qui distinguent les objets ouvrés usuels de ceux qui sont destinés au commerce, car ils constituent aussi un chaînon important entre les traditions historiques et les activités contemporaines. Les objets usuels se caractérisent par leur nature fonctionnelle, plutôt que par leur perfection esthétique. Dans les objets destinés au commerce, on met l'accent sur l'agréable, le diminutif et la représentation exacte des activités humaines et des animaux de l'Arctique, ainsi que des objets importés par les kadlunat. Alors que les objets usuels de cette période sont exécutés d'une façon rudimentaire[5] et manquent de fini, l'art commercial est plus perfectionné. Les objets usuels présentent une esthétique robuste, candide et sans prétention, une forme d'art folklorique et non d'art primitif. Même l'art commercial, bien que plus raffiné et souvent trop badin, conserve une facture nettement folklorique, en dépit de son aspect manifestement commercial.

C'est par son contenu, tiré exclusivement du milieu, que l'art esquimau historique a pris un caractère folklorique. Par art folklorique j'entends une forme d'art conditionnée par le milieu, c'est-à-dire reliée aux idées suggérées par le folklore ou l'expérience directe du milieu, et non par des théories esthétiques élaborées et des allégories complexes de ce qu'on est convenu d'appeler les 'beaux-arts ou arts évolués', ceux-ci ayant habituellement rejeté ou raffiné leurs influences d'origine folklorique.

Les aspects ambivalents de l'art usuel et de l'art commercial, d'une part, et le caractère folklorique, d'autre part, fournissent un lien subtil entre l'art d'aujourd'hui et celui du dix-neuvième siècle. Maintenant, il est évident que la progression rapide de l'acculturation et les répercussions du marché d'art international ont amené un développement plus intensif et complexe.

La rapidité et l'intensité de l'acculturation d'après-guerre a polarisé davantage les différences entre les sculptures rudimentaires et les sculptures commerciales plus raffinées. En même temps, les formes maintenant polarisées ont été perfectionnées par certains artistes comme Johnnie Inukpuk, Kavik, Latcholassie, Pangnark, Pauta, Charlie Seeguarpik, Tasseor et Tiktak, pour n'en nommer que quelques-uns. Et plus récemment, un nombre croissant de sculptures fantaisistes et mythologiques, présentant des aspects grotesques et surréalistes, ont également fait leur apparition; elles sont apparues simultanément à Cape Dorset au début des années soixante (Aggiak, Audla, Axangayuk, Kiawak, Oshooweetook et Saggiak), à Povungnituk au milieu de la décennie (Davideealuk et Eli Salualuk) et tout récemment dans d'autres localités. En fait, il est maintenant possible de reconnaître des profils de croissance bien définis dans diverses régions, selon des séquences qui diffèrent avec les circonstances d'acculturation et d'expansion économique.

Le profil se dessine ainsi: d'abord l'étape rudimentaire (souvent faussement appelée 'primitive') suivie par des raffinements qui conduisent soit au naturalisme, soit à la formalisation. S'il n'y a pas, à ce stade, une évaluation ou une orientation sympathique, plusieurs programmes artistiques s'écroulent, faute d'une exploitation réfléchie de leur propre succès, aboutissant à la production de clichés et de répétitions. Par contre, dans les localités énergiques, certains artistes surgissent; ils apportent des intuitions neuves, introduisant de nouveaux profils de croissance, et déterminent généralement le progrès dans leur localité.

Cependant, à ce stade du développement, la présence de Blancs informés et sympathiques en qualité d'administrateurs de programmes, qu'ils soient commerçants ou résidants, influe considérablement sur le succès du projet et sur l'épanouissement des artistes. C'est avant tout ce facteur qui fait que l'art contemporain se distingue si nettement de l'art de la période historique, alors que chacun était isolé, les progrès ayant lieu à mesure que les sculpteurs apprenaient sporadiquement les goûts des chasseurs de baleines, des explorateurs et des commerçants. Mais comme la sculpture est devenue aujourd'hui une opération lucrative et vu que les prix sont fixés d'après les goûts individuels des commerçants et des administrateurs de programme, les sculpteurs dépendent beaucoup plus des Blancs qui demeurent plus ou moins en permanence dans les communautés. Les artistes de Baker Lake, Dorset, Eskimo Point, Lake Harbour, Port Harrison, Povungnituk, Rankin Inlet et Repulse Bay ont toujours tiré avantage des résidants blancs qui les orientent avec intelligence et sympathie en guidant sans contrôler, en encourageant sans diriger, en inspirant sans commander. De grandes réalisations sont survenues dans ces localités et les artistes esquimaux sont devenus conscients de la nécessité de gérer leurs propres affaires, ainsi que de leurs capacités dans ce domaine.

Ajoutons que certaines communautés comptent des artistes qui travaillent bien quand ils produisent peu ou d'autres qui livrent une excellente production pendant deux ans et s'arrêtent subitement. En cela, ils ne diffèrent pas de maints artistes du monde occidental; il est donc déraisonnable et naïf de s'attendre à un flot constant de grandes réalisations artistiques de la part de tout un peuple. Mais à cause du mythe de l'Esquimau artiste universel, tel est souvent le cas. Au moment même où leur existence culturelle et spirituelle est menacée d'extinction, on demande aux artistes esquimaux de produire des oeuvres dans un langage exprimant et affirmant un mode de vie et une adaptation au milieu nettement anachroniques. Qu'ils réussissent à nous donner une idée de l'existence esquimaude du passé, au lieu d'échouer lamentablement dans cette entreprise, tient du miracle. Leur art ressemble beaucoup au chant du cygne; peut-être plus effroyablement (et même avec plus de beauté) les artistes sont-ils, comme le poète de Kierkegaard, des hommes malheureux qui, dans leur coeur, 'nourrissent une angoisse profonde, mais dont les lèvres sont ainsi faites que les cris et les gémissements qui les franchissent sont transformés en musique enchanteresse . . .'

Sans doute, cette qualité du nouvel art, créé par un peuple qui chante ce qu'il n'est plus, contient-elle un double élément de tragédie et d'ironie: au pire, il reflète une étape dans l'agonie et la mort d'une race; à son meilleur, il révèle davantage ce qui était, et non ce qui est.

En plus du chant du cygne, une autre idée surgit: les nouvelles formes, l'individualité propre des artistes, les techniques qui englobent les structures économiques et les communications modernes, les oeuvres convaincantes qui sont en fait différentes des oeuvres du passé, engendrent des semences et des espoirs permettant d'entrevoir un avenir basé sur un nouveau milieu. Les nouvelles sculptures deviennent une réalité nouvelle.

Comme il est presque impossible de s'entendre sur l'orthographe des noms esquimaux, nous avons donc utilisé autant que possible une orthographe phonétique acceptée par les artistes. L'orthographe choisie a été dictée par les coutumes établies et par des consultations avec les artistes. Il est donc légitime de penser que les noms indiqués en toutes lettres sont

*les noms esquimaux les plus usuels. Les nombres entre parenthèses repré-
sentent les numéros d'enregistrement d'Esquimaux. Nous les avons inscrits
ici pour faciliter l'identification.*

GEORGE SWINTON

NOTES

1 *Prononcé cha-na-ngu-ak et cha-na-ngu-a'-gak.*

2 *Ces subtilités linguistiques ont été longuement étudiées avec MM. R. G. Williamson
et T. C. Corrall.*

3 *R. G. Williamson, 'The Canadian Arctic Sociocultural Change,'* Arch. Environ.
Health, 17 *(Oct. 1968), 484–91.*

4 *Cf. Charles A. Martijn, 'Canadian Eskimo Carving in Historical Perspective,'
Antleropos, LIX (1965), 546–96. Charles A. Martijn, 'A Retrospective Glance,' The
Beaver, 298 (Autumn 1967), 4–19. George Swinton,* Eskimo Sculpture – Sculpture
esquimaude *(McClelland and Stewart, 1965).*

5 *L'emploi des adjectifs 'rudimentaire' et 'primitif' n'implique pas un jugement de
valeur dans le contexte artistique. On dit d'une société qu'elle est 'primitive'
lorsqu'elle n'a subi aucune acculturation, et un art 'primitif' est souvent très complexe, affiné et adroitement exécuté (l'art des Indiens de la côte Nord-Ouest, par
exemple. On dit d'un art qu'il est 'rudimentaire' lorsque la technique manque de
raffinement et de poli, qualités qui n'influent en rien sur le contenu de l'oeuvre,
mais qui souvent la mettent en valeur. De telles oeuvres se signalent souvent par
leur candeur, leur simplicité et l'absence de tape-à-l'oeil. Le public a toujours
méprisé l'art rudimentaire, ce qui a pour effet de promouvoir les formes plus
'respectables' de l'art commercial du dix-neuvième siècle et l'art pour les touristes
du vingtième siècle.*

*Une bonne part de la production contemporaine est destinée au commerce et
aux touristes, ce qui se comprend aisément dans les conditions actuelles d'acculturation. Mais la grande quantité d'oeuvres valables produites en dépit de l'industrie du souvenir ne laisse pas de surprendre. Cette situation n'est d'ailleurs pas
différente de la nôtre, où le cliché prime sur la création dans une proportion beaucoup plus marquée.*

To find life in the stone

Ayii, ayii
I walked on the ice of the sea,
And wondering I heard the song of the sea,
The great sighing of new-formed ice.
Go then go, strength of soul
Bring health to the place of feasting.

ESKIMO SONG

The best Eskimo carvings of all ages seem to possess a powerful ability to reach across the great barriers of language and time and communicate directly with us. The more we look at these carvings, the more life we perceive hidden within them. We discover subtle living forms of the animal, human, and mystical world. These arctic carvings are not the cold sculptures of a frozen world. Instead, they reveal to us the passionate feelings of a vital people well aware of all the joys, terrors, tranquility, and wildness of life around them.

Eskimo carvers are people moved by dreams. In spite of all their new contacts with outsiders, they are still concerned with their own kind of mystical imagery. The most skillful carvers possess a bold confidence, a direct approach to their art that has a special freedom unsullied by any kind of formalized training.

Eskimo carvers have strong skilled hands, used to forcing hard materials with their simple tools. Their hunting life and the northern environment invigorates them. Bad weather often imposes a special kind of leisure, giving them time in which to perfect their carvings.

They are among the last of the hunting societies that have retained some part of the keen sense of observation that we have so long forgotten. The carvers are also butchers of meat, and therefore masters in the understanding of animal anatomy. Flesh and bones and sheaths of muscle seem to move in their works. They show us how to drive the caribou, how to hold a child, how to walk cautiously on thin ice. Through their eyes we understand the dangerous power of a polar bear. In the very best of Eskimo art we see vibrant animal and human forms that stand quietly or tensely, strongly radiating a sense of life. We can see, and even feel with our hands, the cold sleekness of seals, the hulking weight of walrus, the icy swiftness of trout, the flowing rhythm in a flight of geese. In their art we catch brief glimpses of a people who have long possessed a very different approach to the whole question of life and death.

In Eskimo art there is much evidence of humour which the carvers have in abundance. Some of the carvings are caricatures of themselves, of ourselves, and of situations, or records of ancient legends. Their laughter may be subtle, or broad and Chaucerian.

Perhaps no one can accurately define the right way or wrong way to create a carving. Each carver must follow his own way, in his own time. Technique in itself is meaningless unless it serves to express content. According to the Eskimo, the best carvings possess a sense of movement that seems to come from within the material itself, a feeling of tension, a living excitement.

I believe that Eskimos do not have a satisfactory word for art because they have never felt the need for such a term. Like most other hunting societies, they have thought of the whole act of living in harmony with nature as their art. The small objects that they carve or decorate are to them insignificant reflections of their total art of living. They share this belief with the Hopi, the Ainu, and many others. They share the concept that the very act of hunting, of killing for food, is part of a religious act. Why else would they have returned a portion of the walrus liver to the sea, replanted bird's feathers in the snow, given the dead seal a drink of fresh water? Why would some have carried these old ideas into the new era?

In the 1920s the famous Danish ethnologist Knud Rasmussen travelled for some years throughout the Canadian Arctic as leader of the Fifth Thule Expedition. The published findings of the expedition stand as a most important ethnic study of Canadian Eskimos. Specifically Rasmussen's own writings, *Intellectual Culture of the Iglulik Eskimos* (1929), *Intellectual Culture of the Caribou Eskimos* (1930), *The Netsilik Eskimo's Social Life and Spiritual Structure* (1931), and *Intellectual Culture of the Copper Eskimos* (1932), are four volumes that give a true insight into the Eskimo mind and spirit world, and give the background for an understanding of contemporary Eskimo carving.

In 1948 Eskimo carvers in remote camps still lived lives little changed from the time when Rasmussen had travelled among them, for even in his time they knew traders and missionaries. In the 1950s when the building of the DEW line, the intrusion of more outsiders, and the development of villages with school requirements for children, the Eskimos' life style began to change at a more rapid pace, a pace that is accelerating today and will continue to do so with the development of oil and mineral deposits, air travel, and the introduction of industry into the Arctic.

Some say that Eskimos in the twentieth century carve only for commercial reasons. That may be true, if we will admit to ourselves that commercialism has motivated almost all western art down through the centuries. We have admired the wild freedom and genius of those artists who dashed off a sketch or two in exchange for a loaf of bread and a glass of wine in some Paris café, yet no one has ever been able to destroy the romance that surrounded those painters, and few have called them commercial. Rasmussen's words explain perfectly the Eskimo condition that caused the carvers to welcome so readily today's large active trade in carvings.

The quality of some of the work has unquestionably diminished and yet we see some works performed in the 1970s that are as fine as any ever created in the 2800 years of Eskimo carving. At this time Eskimo carving has become like the uneven art of New York, Paris, and London, and the buyer must carefully seek out the best objects.

Good Eskimo carvers create their art freely and often with astonishing originality. These carvers are, of course, willing to trade or sell the objects as artists and craftsmen have always done throughout history. The artist has always parted with his work, to kings, high priests, tribal chiefs, or modern collectors, so that they in turn might glorify their ancestors, their religion, their homes, or even themselves. The act of creating a work of art is the essential thrill of the artist, not the act of retaining it for himself.

The change in the position of Eskimo carvings from rare ethnological objects to art objects for trade purposes may have occurred too swiftly for some, but who would have counselled the Eskimos to wait in the face of our overwhelming onslaught of civilization? Carvings have unquestionably provided an important source of pride and income to many Eskimos in the Canadian Arctic. In trading their carvings, Eskimos living in remote camps and settlements have often obtained trade goods or cash, when no other means was available to them.

These northern people have always utilized a variety of carving materials: walrus ivory, bone, antler, and stone. The Canadian eastern and central Arctic possesses many rich open deposits of semi-soft carving stone. These deposits are usually located along the barren coasts, often below the tide line. Though inaccessible during the dark months of winter, the stone is quarried during the endless days that come with summer. This carving stone, traditionally used for lamps and pots as well as sculpture, differs greatly from area to area, varying from the dark steatite to rich green serpentine, all perfect for the carvers' art. Stone, bone, and ivory are all materials easily polished by hand.

The Eskimo people have recently built their own strong co-operatives, and through them have marketed carvings and stone block prints. By means of these producer co-operatives, the Eskimos begin to share in their country's future, the shaping of their own destiny. This is an essential part of the opening of the Canadian north.

Eskimo carving over the past twenty years has been a passionate affair. A carver at the very height of his fame, with new-found wealth and public appreciation, has often totally ceased to carve for months or even years because of some disenchantment or because the images would not come to him. Suddenly, without explanation, he will start again. Such inspired and uninspired periods are shared by true artists everywhere. This is hardly a commercial approach to carving.

In this collection of contemporary Eskimo art we see the confident hands of the carver plunging into difficult artistic problems with unabashed self assurance. The Eskimo artist attacks these problems with abandon, unfettered by the laws and stylizations that have come to govern most art. This naiveté is his true strength, to understand this fully is to understand the great profusion of carvings and the unevenness of the quality of their work.

Out of this inventiveness, this feverish production of images, something of lasting importance has already emerged. It represents the strongest Eskimo creative spirit of the twentieth century. Look and you will see how well their best contemporary works stand with the carvings of their own past.

The Eskimos may or may not have competitive feelings upon seeing carvings done by their neighbours. Rather than attempting to imitate each other, it is quite evident that they have tried to excel in originality, for they are true innovators.

Jorgen Meldgaard has said of contemporary Canadian carvings in his book *Eskimo Sculpture*, published in Copenhagen (1959) and London and New York (1960): 'With these sculptures Eskimo art had acquired a fresh purpose and a different "social position"; it stands on its own, freed of the traditional ties which in modern times have often restricted the rest of the Eskimos, and made them copyists either of their own past products or of those from the New World. It is significant that this freedom reached the Canadian Eskimos while they were still living like Eskimos. That is why they produce genuine Eskimo art.'

Already we begin to hear from a new generation of young Canadian Eskimos, ones who have been partially exposed to our school system. Surprisingly we find that a number of these students, following their family ways, are real carvers. These young people have learned Canadian ways and speak back to us with thoughts, words, and motives entwined with our own.

The government of Canada recognized the importance of Eskimo art in 1950 and initiated a small grant to allow further development in new areas in the Arctic. Since that time the Canadian goverment has continued to do everything possible to encourage the carvers' art, both in the Arctic and in world sales and exhibitions.

The selection of this exhibition has been an exquisite torture for the selection committee and persons viewing this display of carvings will undoubtedly feel that some important pieces are missing. They are indeed correct, for we have been privileged to choose from an embarrassment of riches.

Today, contemporary Eskimo art is a highly controversial subject. I hope that it will remain so for years to come. Strong controversy indicates that this virile art form remains alive, that it continues to gain the stimulation to grow and develop in Canada.

The Metropolitan Museum of Art in New York in a recent exhibition, *Masterpieces of Fifty Centuries*, showed three contemporary Canadian Eskimo sculptures. They were displayed along with the great works of

Egyptian tomb builders and Greek temple makers, Leonardo da Vinci and Rembrandt, Hokusai and Picasso. It was a heart warming sight to view these three stone carvings of the Arctic, a sea goddess, a seated woman with child, and a wild green bear, all resting in timeless harmony with so many other works of genius.

JAMES HOUSTON

Dégager la vie
emprisonée dans la pierre

Aii, ayii,
J'écoutais en marchant sur la mer gelée
Et je croyais entendre la mélodie de la mer,
Ces grands soupirs de la glace fraîchement durcie,
Avance, ô force de l'âme,
Répands la santé au milieu de la fête.

CHANT ESQUIMAU

Les meilleures sculptures esquimaudes de tous les temps semblent pos-
séder le pouvoir de franchir les obstacles du langage et du temps pour
communiquer directement avec nous. Plus nous les observons, plus nous
y découvrons de vie. Elles nous révèlent des subtilités du monde animal,
humain ou mystique. Ces sculptures de l'Arctique sont loin d'être froides.
Au contraire, elles nous révèlent les sentiments passionnés d'un peuple
bien conscient des joies, des terreurs, de la tranquillité et de l'isolement
dont est faite leur vie quotidienne.
Le sculpteur esquimau est imprégne de rêves. En dépit de ses nouveaux
contacts avec des personnes étrangères à sa race, il continue de faire revi-
vre sa propre imagerie mystique. L'artiste digne de ce nom a une con-
fiance audacieuse, une simplicité d'expression alliée à une certaine liberté
exempte de formalisme acquis.

La dextérité du sculpteur esquimau se cache dans une grosse main forte, habituée à vaincre la dureté des matériaux avec des outils simples. Les péripéties de sa vie de chasseur dans un milieu rude contribuent à sa vigueur. Les intempéries du climat lui imposent des moments prolongés de loisir, qu'il consacre à perfectionner ses oeuvres.

Appartenant à l'une des dernières races de chasseurs, il est nanti de ce sens aigu de l'observation qui devient de plus en plus rare de nos jours. En dépeçant son gibier, il acquiert une connaissance plus exacte de l'anatomie d'un animal. Chair, os et muscles semblent s'animer dans ses oeuvres. Il nous montre comment conduire un caribou, comme tenir un enfant, comment marcher avec précaution sur une mince couche de glace. Ses yeux ont saisi pour nous la dangereuse puissance de l'ours blanc. Dans les meilleures oeuvres esquimaudes, nous retrouvons la vie palpitante des humains et des animaux à l'état de détente ou de tension, mais toujours rayonnant de vitalité. A la vue comme au toucher, nous sommes impressionnés par l'apparence profilée du phoque, le poids énorme du morse, le frétillement de la truite ou encore le rythme fuyant d'une volée d'oies. Nous décelons dans les oeuvres esquimaudes une conception différente, d'ailleurs très ancienne, de la vie et de la mort.

L'art esquimau révèle de nombreuses manifestations de l'humour qui foisonne dans l'esprit des artistes. Certaines sculptures représentent un des leurs ou un des nôtres, une situation particulière ou un souvenir venant d'une vieille légende. L'allusion est tantôt subtile, tantôt crue et grivoise.

Il est difficile de s'entendre sur la meilleure manière de créer une sculpture. Chacun suit son intuition au moment où cela lui plaît. La technique en soi est inutile, si elle ne sert à exprimer un contenu. Pour les Esquimaux, la meilleure sculpture est imprégnée d'un mouvement qui jaillit de la matière avec une tension sensible, une exubérance de vie.

Si les Exquimaux n'ont pas de terme pour exprimer l'art, c'est qu'ils n'ont jamais senti le besoin d'en parler. Comme les autres peuples de chasseurs, ils ont toujours pensé que la vie en harmonie avec la nature était un art en soi. Les petits objets sculptés ou décorés par leurs soins leur paraissent des reflets ordinaires de leur bonheur de vivre. Sur ce point, ils rejoignent les Hopis, les Ainus et nombre d'autres peuples primitifs. Comme eux, ils sont convaincus que le geste du chasseur qui tue pour sa subsistance est partie intégrante d'un geste religieux. On ne peut s'expliquer autrement leurs coutumes consistant à jeter à la mer une partie du foie du morse, à piquer des plumes d'oiseaux dans la neige, à donner une rasade d'eau fraîche au phoque abattu. Quelle autre signification donner à la conservation de ces gestes parmi les habitudes plus nouvelles?

Au cours des années 1920, le célèbre ethnologue danois, Knud Rasmussen, a parcouru l'Arctique canadien durant plusieurs années en qualité de chef de la cinquième expédition de Thulé. Le récit des constatations relevées pendant l'expédition demeurent une étude ethnique remarquable sur les Esquimaux du Canada. Les quatre volumes des écrits de Rasmussen, intitulés Intellectual Culture of the Iglulik Eskimos (1929), Intellectual Culture of the Caribou Eskimos (1930), The Netsilik Eskimo's Social Life and Spiritual Structure (1931), et Intellectual Culture of the Copper Eskimos (1932), donnent un aperçu fidèle de l'esprit et de la mentalité des Esquimaux, tout en brossant un tableau permettant de mieux saisir le sens de leurs sculptures contemporaines.

Les sculpteurs esquimaux des centres éloignés vivaient encore en 1948 comme au temps des voyages de Rasmussen. Les Esquimaux connaissaient déjà les commerçants et les missionnaires. Avec la construction des stations du réseau avancé de pré-alerte (DEW) vers 1950, l'intrusion des étrangers, ainsi que l'aménagement de villages et des installations scolaires, ont amené un nouveau mode de vie chez les Esquimaux. Cette évolution continue de s'accentuer avec l'exploitation des ressources pétrolières et minières, le développement du transport aérien et l'implantation de l'industrie dans l'Arctique.

D'aucuns disent que les Esquimaux du vingtième siècle s'adonnent à la sculpture pour des raisons commerciales. Cette constatation est peut-être vraie, mais il faut se rappeler que ce fut le motif qui a inspiré tous les arts occidentaux à travers les siècles. Nous étions remplis d'admiration pour le génie artistique de ceux qui créaient une esquisse ou deux en échange d'un pain et d'un verre de vin dans certains cafés de Paris. L'esprit romantique qui entourait ce geste lui enlevait toute vénalité. Rasmussen décrit bien la mentalité des Esquimaux, qui dispose les sculpteurs à profiter sans arrière-pensée de la grande vogue de leurs sculptures.

Il est indiscutable que la qualité des oeuvres baisse. On trouve, cependant, parmi les pièces exécutées en 1970, des oeuvres qui ont autant de classe que toute autre création des 2,800 années de sculpture esquimaude. Nous en sommes au point où l'amateur de sculpture esquimaude doit opérer un choix méticuleux des meilleures oeuvres avant d'acheter, tout comme on doit le faire pour les oeuvres de valeur inégale venant de New-York, Paris ou Londres.

Les bons sculpteurs esquimaux produisent librement leurs oeuvres d'une façon très originale. Les artistes véritables se sont toujours séparés du fruit de leur travail au profit des rois, des grands-prêtres, des chefs de la tribu ou des collectionneurs modernes, qui cherchaient à glorifier leurs ancêtres, leur religion, leurs demeures, voire leur propre personne. La création d'une oeuvre d'art remplit l'artiste d'un plaisir personnel, sans le porter à la conserver pour son propre usage. Comme les artistes et artisans du monde, les sculpteurs esquimaux consentent à échanger ou à vendre leurs oeuvres.

La transition fut trop brusque, au dire de certains, entre le temps où les sculptures esquimaudes n'étaient que des pièces ethnologiques et celui où elles sont devenues des pièces d'art mises sur le marché. Qui aurait pu conseiller aux Esquimaux d'attendre, alors que notre civilisation les envahit? La sculpture a constitué, sans aucun doute, une grande source de fierté et de revenus pour plus d'un Esquimau de l'Arctique. Ceux qui habitent des centres isolés ont obtenu en retour des articles ou de l'argent, chose impossible auparavant.

Ces sculpteurs du Nord ont toujours utilisé des matériaux divers: l'ivoire du morse, des morceaux d'os, d'andouiller ou de pierre. Le sol canadien de l'est ou du centre de l'Arctique renferme plusieurs gisements ouverts de pierre semi-tendre propre à la sculpture. On les retrouve ordinairement le long des rives dénudées et même sous la laisse de haute mer. C'est au cours des journées interminables de l'été qu'on extrait la pierre inaccessible durant la noirceur des mois d'hiver. Cette pierre utilisée traditionnellement tant pour des lampes et des pots que pour les pièces sculptées, diffère d'un endroit à l'autre, variant de la stéatite foncée à la serpentine verte, mais elle se prête toujours parfaitement à l'exécution d'oeuvres d'art. La pierre, l'os et l'ivoire sont tous des éléments faciles à polir à la main.

Depuis peu, les Esquimaux ont créé leurs solides coopératives, aux fins d'écouler leurs sculptures et leurs estampes. Grâce à ces coopératives de production, les Esquimaux bénéficient déjà de l'élan prometteur de leur pays et peuvent se refaire une destinée particulière. Nous croyons que cette évolution est essentielle à l'expansion du Nord canadien.

Au cours des vingt dernières années, l'art esquimau a obéi à des impulsions mystérieuses. Un sculpteur célèbre, nouvellement riche et choyé du public, cesse de travailler pendant des mois, parfois même des années, par désenchantement ou par absence d'inspiration. Soudain, sans aucune explication, il reprend son outil et se met à l'oeuvre. C'est le lot des véritables artistes de tous lieux d'avoir des périodes creuses; on ne saurait qualifier cela de comportement commercial.

Dans la présente collection d'art esquimau contemporain, nous pouvons déceler le geste confiant du sculpteur qui s'aventure dans des domaines artistiques difficiles avec la plus haute assurance. En les attaquant, il se dégage des craintes ou contraintes imposées ordinairement par les règlements et les styles qui régentent les arts. Quand on songe que sa force réside dans sa naïveté, on s'étonne moins de la profusion des oeuvres et de leur valeur inégale.

Dans ce flot d'imagination et de production, on découvre déjà des pièces qui ont les caractéristiques d'une oeuvre durable et qui perpétueront l'esprit créateur des Esquimaux du vingtième siècle. A l'observation, on constate que leurs meilleures pièces contemporaires soutiennent la comparaison avec les chefs-d'oeuvre des années antérieures.

Il n'est pas sûr que les Esquimaux ressentent l'aiguillon de la concurrence en voyant les oeuvres de leurs émules. Ils ne prennent manifestement pas leur inspiration chez leurs confrères; ils désirent, au contraire, exceller dans l'originalité, car ils sont de véritables innovateurs.

Dans son livre intitulé Eskimo Sculpture, publié à Copenhague en 1959 et à Londres et New-York en 1960, Jorgen Meldgaard a fait les remarques suivantes au sujet des sculptures contemporaines du Canada: 'Par ces sculptures, l'art esquimau a pris une orientation nouvelle et une position sociale différente; il acquiert une dimension personnelle, en se libérant des liens traditionnels qui avaient souvent conduit les Esquimaux à copier les oeuvres de leurs devanciers ou celles du Nouveau-Monde. Ce n'est pas par hasard que les Esquimaux canadiens se sont libérés, alors qu'ils vivent encore à la façon esquimaude. C'est la raison de l'authenticité de leur art.'

Nous commençons déjà à entendre parler de la jeune génération, qui a été partiellement mêlée à notre culture dans nos écoles. A notre grande surprise, nous découvrons qu'un bon nombre de ces jeunes sont de vrais sculpteurs, qui s'inspirent de leur vie familiale. Ayant appris à vivre comme nous, ils s'expriment par des pensées, des expressions et des motifs qui s'entremêlent avec les nôtres.

Le gouvernement du Canada a reconnu la valeur de l'art esquimau en 1950, prenant même l'initiative d'accorder une modeste subvention destinée à promouvoir la création artistique dans de nouvelles régions de l'Arctique. Depuis cette date, le gouvernement canadien a multiplié ses encouragements envers la sculpture artistique, tant dans l'Arctique que dans les divers coins du monde où l'on vend ou expose des oeuvres esquimaudes.

Le choix des pièces d'exposition a été très embarrassant pour le comité de sélection. Plusieurs visiteurs trouveront, à juste titre, des vides dans la collection. De fait, il nous a fallu faire un choix parmi un grand nombre d'oeuvres remarquables.

L'art esquimau contemporain prête le flanc à la controverse. J'espère qu'il en sera ainsi pendant encore plusieurs années. Les divergences d'opinions prouvent que cet art viril est bien vivant et continue de recevoir des stimulants qui favoriseront son essor.

Parmi les oeuvres présentées par le Métropolitan Museum of Art de New-York lors d'une récente exposition intitulée Masterpieces of Fifty Centuries, figuraient trois sculptures contemporaines de l'art esquimau canadien: une déesse de la mer, une femme assise avec un enfant et un ours vert. Elles voisinaient avec les chefs-d'oeuvre de l'art funéraire égyptien et de l'architecture grecque, aux côtés des toiles de Léonard de Vinci, de Rembrandt, de Picasso et des gravures de Hokusaï. Il faisait chaud au coeur de voir ces trois sculptures de l'Arctique se marier en une parfaite harmonie avec de nombreuses autres oeuvres de génie.

JAMES HOUSTON

Colour Portfolio / Section en couleur

In this catalogue the description of materials used is confined to simple terms such as, stone, bone, ivory, etc. This was done to avoid technical confusions which highly specific geological and biological terms might have introduced. Such terms would be more exact, but, usually, they are only more relevant to scientists and not to art viewers. The measurements given are in centimeters and are in the following order:
height, width, depth.

Dans le présent catalogue, la description des matériaux utilisés a été restreinte à des termes simples tels que pierre, os, ivoire, afin d'éviter toute confusion d'ordre technique qu'aurait pu entraîner l'emploi de termes géologiques et biologiques très précis. Certes plus exacts que les premiers, ces termes auraient été plus appropriés si le catalogue avait été destiné à des scientistes plutôt qu'à des amateurs d'art. Les dimensions sont données en centimètres et en l'ordre suivant:
hauteur, largeur, profondeur.

40
Clothed female doll *Poupée féminine habillée*
Artist unknown *Artiste inconnu*
Cumberland Sound *Baie Cumberland*
Before 1900 *Avant 1900*
Wood, skin and beads *Bois, peau et perles de verre*
9.5 x 4 x 1.5

54
Comb with face *Peigne avec visage*
Dorset culture *Culture de Dorset*
Maxwell Bay, south of Devon Island *Baie Maxwell, sud de l'île Devon*
Ivory *Ivoire*
6.3 x 2.5 x 0.7

106
Fisherman carrying his catch *Pêcheur portant sa prise*
Oogark, Fabien 1923–
Pelly Bay
1964
Ivory *Ivoire*
8.5 x 4 x 3

120
Polar bear *Ours blanc*
Kittosuk, Charlie 1927–
Belcher Islands *Iles Belcher*
1966
Grey-green stone *Pierre vert-de-gris*
17 X 12.5 X 9.5

158
Bear *Ours*
Pauta 1916–
Cape Dorset
1964
Black stone and ivory *Pierre noire et ivoire*
43 x 36 x 35

174
Owl *Harfang*
Qirluaq 1950–
Repulse Bay
ca. 1968
Grey-green mottled stone *Pierre marbrée de vert-de-gris*
15.5 x 12.5 x 7.5

243
Woman with bowl *Femme avec bol*
Tiktak 1916–
Rankin Inlet
1963
Black stone *Pierre noire*
18 x 13 x 17

260

Mother and child with fish *Mère et enfant avec un poisson*
Artist unknown *Artiste inconnu*
Inoucdjouac (Port Harrison)
ca. 1953
Dark green and orange stone and ivory *Pierre vert foncé et orange, et ivoire*
26 x 20 x 26

342

Sea goddess riding a seal *Déesse de la mer à cheval sur un phoque*
Niviaksiak 1908–1959
Cape Dorset
1958
Dark grey-green stone *Pierre vert-de-gris foncé*
9 X 19 X 7

344
Howling spirit (Tornrak) and its young *Esprit hurlant avec son petit*
Kiawak 1933–
Cape Dorset
1962
Green stone *Pierre verte*
24 X 22 X 11

37²
Doll's face *Visage de poupée*
Kiawak 1933–
Cape Dorset
1960
Whale bone *Os de baleine*
13 x 12 x 3

Catalogue/Le catalogue

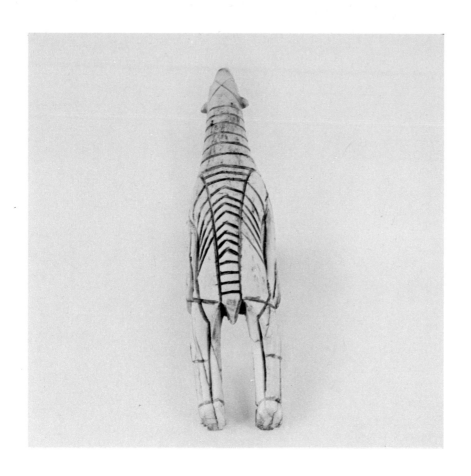

I
Bear *Ours*
Dorset culture *Culture de Dorset*
Alarnerk, Igloolik area *Région d'Igloolik*
Ivory *Ivoire*
3.2 x 15.7 x 3.6

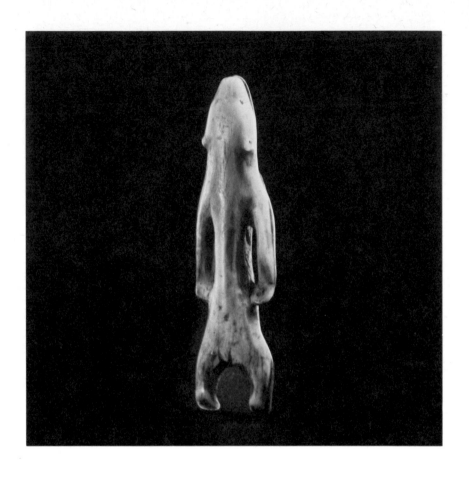

2
Bear *Ours*
Dorset culture *Culture de Dorset*
Igloolik area *Région d'Igloolik*
Ivory *Ivoire*
0.7 x 4.5 x 1.3

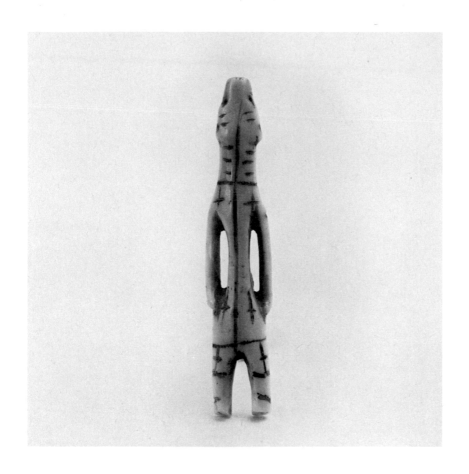

3
Bear *Ours*
Dorset culture *Culture de Dorset*
Ivory *Ivoire*
0.8 x 6.5 x 1.25

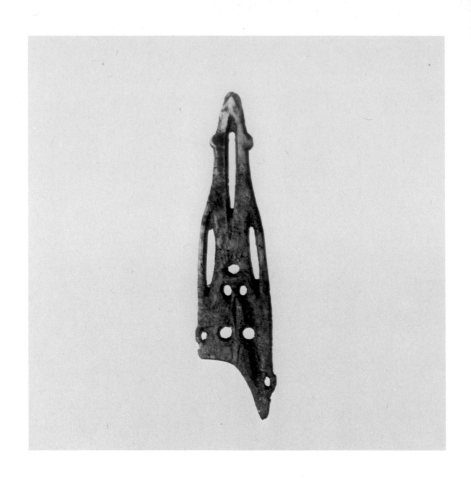

4

Skeletal bear *Ours squelettique*
Dorset culture *Culture de Dorset*
Button Point site, SE tip of Bylot Island
Site de la Pointe Button, à l'extrémité sud-est de l'île Bylot
Ivory *Ivoire*
0.3 x 6.1 x 1.5

5
Skeletal bear *Ours squelettique*
Dorset culture *Culture de Dorset*
Button Point site, SE tip of Bylot Island
Site de la Pointe Button, à l'extrémité sud-est de l'île Bylot
Ivory *Ivoire*
0.35 x 7.85 x 1.5

6

Bear's head (toggle) *Tête d'ours (cabillot)*
Thule culture *Culture de Thulé*
Igloolik
Ivory *Ivoire*
1.65 x 4.2 x 1.95

7
Skeletal seal *Phoque squelettique*
Dorset culture *Culture de Dorset*
Igloolik
Ivory *Ivoire*
2.5 x 1 x 0.7

8

Skeletal bear *Ours squelettique*
Dorset culture *Culture de Dorset*
Button Point site, SE tip of Bylot Island
Site de la Pointe Button, à l'extrémité sud-est de l'île Bylot
Ivory *Ivoire*
0.25 X 6.45 X 0.9

9
Bear's head (or walrus?) *Tête d'ours (ou de morse?)*
Dorset culture *Culture de Dorset*
Mansel Island *Ile Mansel*
Ivory *Ivoire*
0.65 x 4.4 x 0.9

IO

Bear *Ours*
Dorset culture *Culture de Dorset*
Belcher Islands *Iles Belcher*
Ivory *Ivoire*
1.5 X 12 X 3

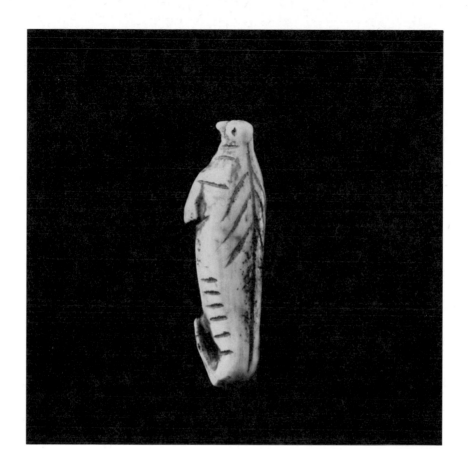

II

Walrus *Morse*
Dorset culture *Culture de Dorset*
Igloolik area *Région d'Igloolik*
Ivory *Ivoire*
0.8 x 3.5 x 1

12

Bear *Ours*
Dorset culture *Culture de Dorset*
Tyara site, Sugluk *Site de Tyara, Saglouc*
Ivory *Ivoire*
0.9 x 5.1 x 1.6

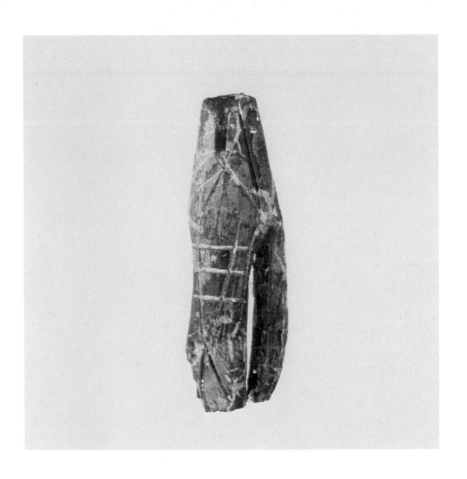

13

Bear *Ours*
Dorset culture *Culture de Dorset*
Tyara site, Sugluk *Site de Tyara, Saglouc*
Ivory *Ivoire*
0.85 x 3.75 x 1.2

I4

Needle case *Etui à aiguilles*
Dorset culture *Culture de Dorset*
Tyara site, Sugluk *Site de Tyara, Saglouc*
Ivory *Ivoire*
1.5 x 7.3 x 2.7

15

Bear fragment *Ours (fragment)*
Dorset culture *Culture de Dorset*
Tyara site, Sugluk *Site de Tyara, Saglouc*
Ivory *Ivoire*
0.45 x 3.1 x 0.95

16
Twin cubs (needle case handle) *Oursons jumeaux (anse d'étui à aiguilles)*
Thule culture *Culture de Thulé*
Igloolik
Ivory *Ivoire*
0.8 x 3.15 x 1.15

17
Animal? *Animal?*
Dorset culture *Culture de Dorset*
Buchanan site, s bank of Ekalluk River
Site Buchanan, rive sud de la rivière Ekalluk
Bone *Os*
1.3 x 5.4 x 0.7

18

Spirit *Esprit*
Dorset culture *Culture de Dorset*
Mill Island (Hudson Strait) *Ile Mill (détroit d'Hudson)*
Ivory *Ivoire*
2.3 x 1.3 x 2.1

19
Double swans *Paire de cygnes*
Dorset culture *Culture de Dorset*
Mansel Island *Ile Mansel*
Ivory *Ivoire*
1 x 6.1 x 2.3

20

Swan *Cygne*
Dorset culture *Culture de Dorset*
Mansel Island *Ile Mansel*
Ivory *Ivoire*
2.2 x 4.2 x 0.8

2I

Bird *Oiseau*
Dorset culture *Culture de Dorset*
Mansel Island *Ile Mansel*
Ivory *Ivoire*
0.8 x 4.75 x 1.3

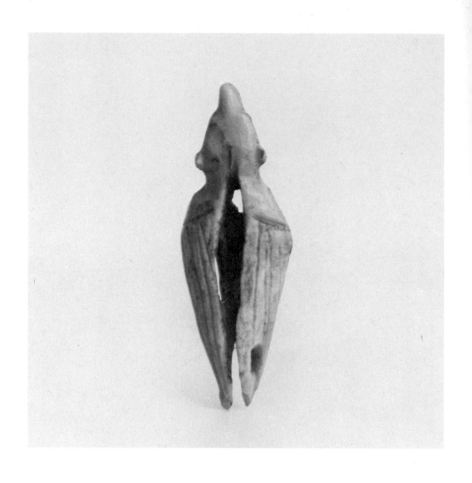

2 2
Bear *Ours*
Dorset culture *Culture de Dorset*
Mill Island (Hudson Strait) *Ile Mill (détroit d'Hudson)*
Ivory *Ivoire*
0.9 x 4.8 x 1.65

23
Falcon *Faucon*
Dorset culture *Culture de Dorset*
Igloolik area *Région d'Igloolik*
Ivory *Ivoire*
0.7 x 4.2 x 1.5

24

Dressed female figure *Femme costumée*
Artist unknown *Artiste inconnue*
Before 1928 *Avant 1928*
Ivory *Ivoire*
13 X 2.7 X 1.3

25
Seated man *Homme assis*
Artist unknown *Artiste inconnu*
Northern Quebec *Nouveau-Québec*
Before 1930 *Avant 1930*
Ivory *Ivoire*
3 x 1.5 x 2.5

26

Female doll *Poupée féminine*
Cumberland Sound *Baie Cumberland*
Before 1900 *Avant 1900*
Wood *Bois*
11.8 x 2.8 x 3

27
Man *Homme*
Thule culture *Culture de Thulé*
Koodlooktook Bay of God's Mercy, Southampton Island
Baie God's Mercy, île Southampton
Ivory *Ivoire*
8.6 x 1.65 x 0.9

28

Woman *Femme*
Artist unknown *Artiste inconnu*
Repulse Bay
1964–65
Ivory *Ivoire*
3.5 x 2 x 1.3

29
Seated figure *Personnage assis*
Artist unknown *Artiste inconnu*
Location unknown *Endroit inconnu*
Before 1930 *Avant 1930*
Ivory *Ivoire*
3 x 1 x 1.5

30
Clothed female doll *Poupée féminine habillée*
Artist unknown *Artiste inconnu*
Central Canadian Arctic *Arctique central du Canada*
Before 1923 *Avant 1923*
Wood and skin *Bois et peau*
6.5 x 3 x 1.5

31
Female doll *Poupée féminine*
Thule culture *Culture de Thulé*
Pond Inlet
Wood *Bois*
1.8 x 3.4 x 1.8

32
Female doll *Poupée féminine*
Thule culture *Culture de Thulé*
Southwest Banks Island *Sud-ouest de l'île Banks*
Wood *Bois*
12.2 X 4.9 X 2.7

33
Figurine *Figurine*
Thule culture *Culture de Thulé*
Igloolik
Stone *Pierre*
5.3 X 1.45 X 0.4

34
Figurine *Figurine*
Thule culture *Culture de Thulé*
Manertog (Steensby Inlet) *(inlet Steensby)*
Antler *Andouiller*
4.55 X 1.54 X 0.35

35
Figurine *Figurine*
Dorset culture *Culture de Dorset*
Igloolik
Stone *Pierre*
2.8 x 1 x 0.6

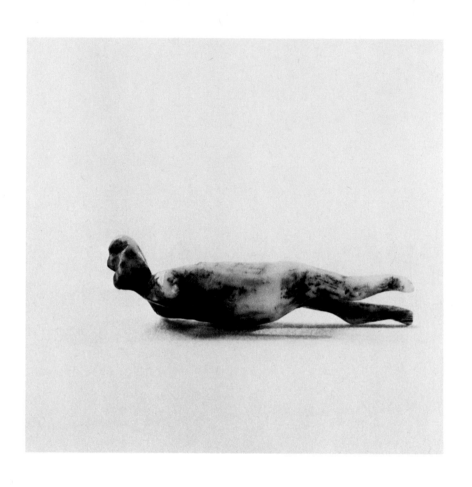

36
Man *Homme*
Dorset culture *Culture de Dorset*
Igloolik area *Région d'Igloolik*
Ivory *Ivoire*
0.8 x 3 x 0.8

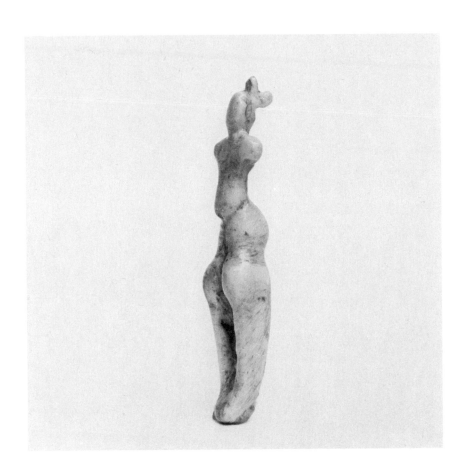

37
Female figure *Personnage féminin*
Thule culture *Culture de Thulé*
Manertog (Steensby Inlet) *(inlet Steensby)*
Ivory *Ivoire*
4.35 x 0.9 x 0.6

38
Seal man *Homme-phoque*
Dorset culture *Culture de Dorset*
Nuvuk Island, Ungava *Ile Nuvuk, Ungave*
Ivory *Ivoire*
1.1 X 3.5 X 1.2

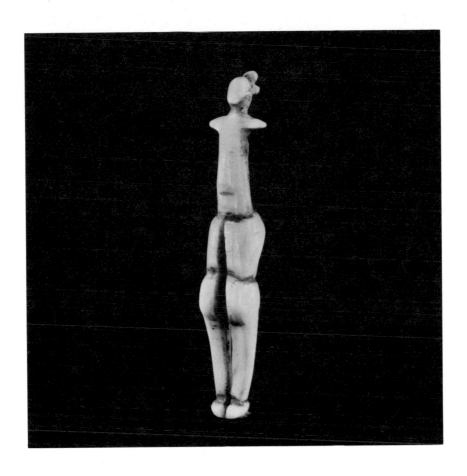

39
Female figure *Personnage féminin*
Thule culture *Culture de Thulé*
Igloolik area *Région d'Igloolik*
Ivory *Ivoire*
5.4 X 1 X 0.7

40

Clothed female doll *Poupée féminine habillée*
Artist unknown *Artiste inconnu*
Cumberland Sound *Baie Cumberland*
Before 1900 *Avant 1900*
Wood, skin and beads *Bois, peau et perles de verre*
9.5 x 4 x 1.5

41
Clothed male figure *Personnage masculin habillé*
Artist unknown *Artiste inconnu*
Eastern Canadian Arctic *Est de l'Arctique canadien*
ca. 1877
Ivory and sealskin *Ivoire et peau de phoque*
4 X 1.5 X 1.3

42

Female doll *Poupée féminine*
Thule culture *Culture de Thulé*
North side Strathcona Sound *Côte nord de la baie Strathcona*
Wood *Bois*
8.8 x 3 x 2

43
Female doll *Poupée féminine*
Thule culture *Culture de Thulé*
Pond Inlet
Wood *Bois*
14.7 x 3.8 x 2

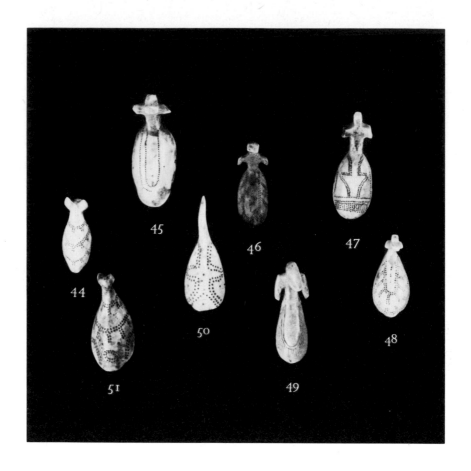

44

Animal (game piece) *Animal (employé dans des jeux occultes)*
Thule culture *Culture de Thulé*
Alarnerk, Igloolik area *Région d'Igloolik*
Ivory *Ivoire*
1.5 x 3 x 1.2

45

Female figure (game piece)
Personnage féminin (employé dans des jeux occultes)
Thule culture *Culture de Thulé*
Igloolik area *Région d'Igloolik*
Ivory *Ivoire*
2.2 X 0.5 X 1.9

46

Female figure (game piece)
Personnage féminin (employé dans des jeux occultes)
Thule culture *Culture de Thulé*
Igloolik area *Région d'Igloolik*
Ivory *Ivoire*
1.6 X 3.7 X 1.4

47

Male figure (game piece)
Personnage masculin (employé dans des jeux occultes)
Thule culture *Culture de Thulé*
Igloolik area *Région d'Igloolik*
Ivory *Ivoire*
1.8 X 4.8 X 1.7

48

Female figure (game piece)
Personnage féminin (employé dans des jeux occultes)
Thule culture *Culture de Thulé*
Igloolik area *Région d'Igloolik*
Ivory *Ivoire*
2 X 3.2 X 1.5

49

Female figure (game piece)
Personnage féminin (employé dans des jeux occultes)
Thule culture *Culture de Thulé*
Igloolik area *Région d'Igloolik*
Ivory *Ivoire*
2 X 4 X 1.3

50

Loon (game piece) *Huart (employé dans des jeux occultes)*
Thule culture *Culture de Thulé*
Igloolik area *Région d'Igloolik*
Ivory *Ivoire*
1.5 X 4.8 X 1.7

51

Head (game piece) *Tête (employé dans des jeux occultes)*
Thule culture *Culture de Thulé*
Igloolik area *Région d'Igloolik*
Ivory *Ivoire*
1.9 X 4 X 1.8

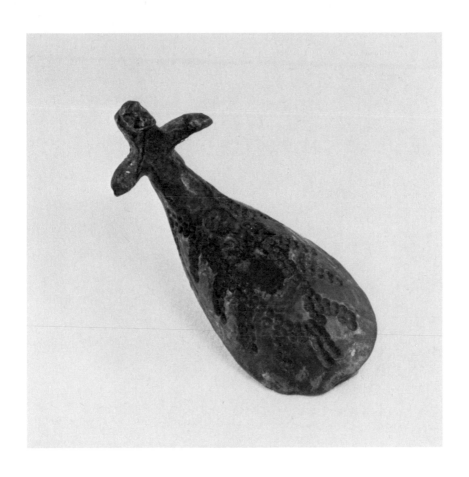

52
Female figure (game piece)
Personnage féminin (employé dans des jeux occultes)
Thule culture *Culture de Thulé*
Pingitkalik (Melville Peninsula) *(Presqu'île Melville)*
Ivory *Ivoire*
1.2 x 3.15 x 1.4

53

Female figure (game piece) *Personnage féminin (employé dans des jeux occultes)*
Thule culture *Culture de Thulé*
Mingooktook (Frobisher Bay) *(baie Frobisher)*
Ivory *Ivoire*
2.9 x 5 x 2.25

54
Comb with face *Peigne avec visage*
Dorset culture *Culture de Dorset*
Maxwell Bay, south of Devon Island *Baie Maxwell, sud de l'île Devon*
Ivory *Ivoire*
6.3 x 2.5 x 0.7

55
Circle of figures *Cercle de personnages*
Artist unknown *Artiste inconnu*
Eastern Canadian Arctic *Est de l'Arctique canadien*
Before 1914 *Avant 1914*
Ivory *Ivoire*
4.7 x 6.3 x 4

56

Marrow pick *Tire-moëlle*
Thule culture *Culture de Thulé*
North side Strathcona Sound *Côte nord de la baie Strathcona*
Ivory *Ivoire*
1.9 X 20.4 X 2.7

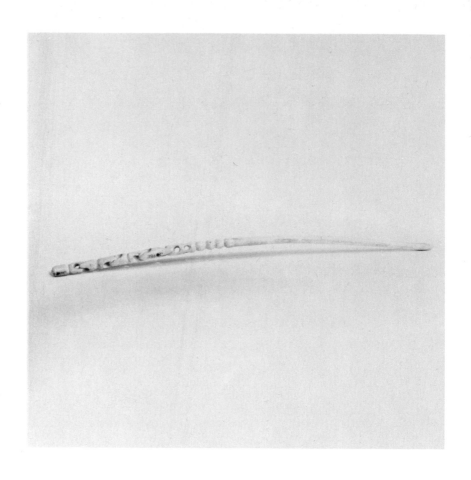

57
Carved object (pin?) *Objet sculpté (épingle?)*
Artist unknown *Artiste inconnu*
North Baffin Island *Nord de l'île Baffin*
Before 1930 *Avant 1930*
Ivory *Ivoire*
1 X 30 X 2

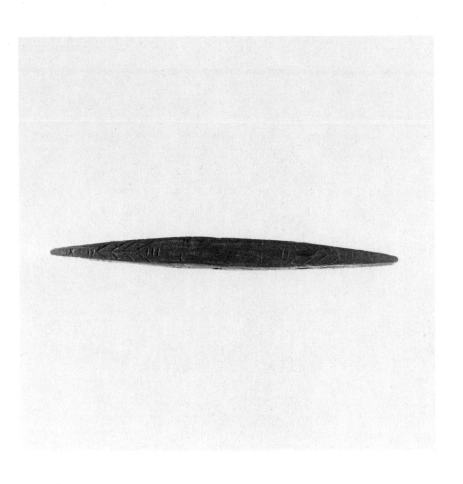

58
Kayak or Bear *Kayak ou ours*
Dorset culture *Culture de Dorset*
Button Point site, SE tip of Bylot Island
Site de la Pointe Button, à l'extrémité sud-est de l'île Bylot
Wood *Bois*
0.9 X 21.5 X 2

59
Two-man pendant *Pendentif à deux hommes*
Thule culture *Culture de Thulé*
Ivory *Ivoire*
4.6 X 2.35 X 1.05

60

Female figure (pendant) *Personnage féminin (pendentif)*
Thule culture *Culture de Thulé*
Levesque Harbour, NE Boothia *Havre Lévesque, nord-est de la presqu-île de Boothia*
Ivory *Ivoire*
5.5 X 2 X 1

61

Engraved baton *Bâton gravé*
Thule culture *Culture de Thulé*
Igloolik
Ivory *Ivoire*
2.05 x 17.75 x 2.3

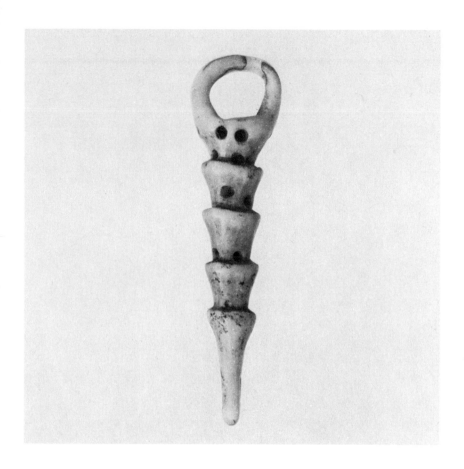

62

Ornament *Ornement*
Thule culture *Culture de Thulé*
Maxwell Bay (South Devon Island) *Baie Maxwell (sud de l'île Devon)*
Ivory *Ivoire*
0.9 x 5.6 x 1.35

63
Seal? (amulet) *Phoque? (amulette)*
Dorset culture *Culture de Dorset*
Port aux Choix – site 2, Newfoundland *Port aux Choix – site 2, Terre-Neuve*
Bone? *Os?*
8.5 x 2.8 x 0.1

64

Ornament *Ornement*
Dorset culture *Culture de Dorset*
Mansel Island *Ile Mansel*
Ivory *Ivoire*
3.95 x 6.55 x 0.25

65
Ornament *Ornement*
Thule culture *Culture de Thulé*
Belcher Islands *Iles Belcher*
Ivory *Ivoire*
1.9 x 4.65 x 0.3

66

Comb bridge? *Dos de peigne?*
Dorset culture *Culture de Dorset*
Mansel Island *Ile Mansel*
Ivory *Ivoire*
3.2 x 1.7 x 0.35

67
Comb *Peigne*
Thule culture *Culture de Thulé*
Sleeper Islands *Iles Sleeper*
Ivory *Ivoire*
12 X 4.55 X 0.55

68
Comb *Peigne*
Thule culture *Culture de Thulé*
Pelly Bay (Isortuk)
Ivory *Ivoire*
11 x 4

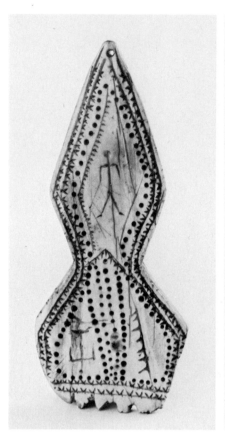
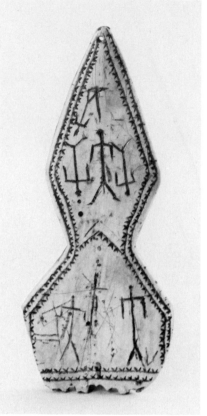

69

Engraved comb bridge *Dos de peigne gravé*
Thule culture *Culture de Thulé*
Igloolik
Ivory *Ivoire*
10.4 x 4.3 x 0.6

70
Hawk *Buse*
Thule culture *Culture de Thulé*
Cape Dorset
Ivory *Ivoire*
2.6 x 1.8 x 3.5

71
Bird *Oiseau*
Dorset culture *Culture de Dorset*
Mill Island (Hudson Strait) *Ile Mill (détroit d'Hudson)*
Ivory *Ivoire*
2.5 x 3.2 x 1.2

72

Snowy Owl *Harfang des neiges*
Dorset culture *Culture de Dorset*
Igloolik area *Région d'Igloolik*
Bone *Os*
2.5 x 3.8 x 2.1

73

Bird in flight *Oiseau en vol*

Artist unknown *Artiste inconnu*

Hebron (Labrador)

Before 1912 *Avant 1912*

Ivory *Ivoire*

0.5 x 3.5 x 2

74
Bird in flight *Oiseau en vol*
Artist unknown *Artiste inconnu*
Hebron (Labrador)
Before 1912 *Avant 1912*
Ivory *Ivoire*
1.5 x 4 x 4

75
Hare *Lièvre*
Artist unknown *Artiste inconnu*
North Baffin Island *Nord de l'île Baffin*
Before 1930 *Avant 1930*
Ivory *Ivoire*
3.2 x 5 x 1.3

76
Weasel *Belette*
Dorset culture *Culture de Dorset*
Pingerluk, east coast Melville Peninsula
Pingerluk, Côte orientale de la presqu'île Melville
Ivory *Ivoire*
1.7 X 5.7 X 1

77

Bear *Ours*
Artist unknown *Artiste inconnu*
Location unknown *Endroit inconnu*
Before 1946 *Avant 1946*
Ivory *Ivoire*
1.3 x 2.5 x 0.7

78

Bear *Ours*
Artist unknown *Artiste inconnu*
Central Canadian Arctic *Arctique central du Canada*
Before 1915 *Avant 1915*
Bone *Os*
1.5 x 3.5 x 1

79
Bear *Ours*
Artist unknown *Artiste inconnu*
Location unknown *Endroit inconnu*
Before 1928 *Avant 1928*
Ivory *Ivoire*
3.9 x 10.7 x 2.5

80

Bear *Ours*
Artist unknown *Artiste inconnu*
Aivilik
Before 1899 *Avant 1899*
Ivory *Ivoire*
2 x 5.8 x 1

81

Dog *Chien*
Artist unknown *Artiste inconnu*
North Baffin Island *Nord de l'île Baffin*
Before 1930 *Avant 1930*
Ivory *Ivoire*
2 x 6 x 1

82

Bear *Ours*
Dorset culture *Culture de Dorset*
Nuvuk Island, Ungava *Ile Nuvuk, Ungave*
Ivory *Ivoire*
0.9 x 1.65 x 0.65

83

Harpooned walrus *Morse harponné*
Artist unknown *Artiste inconnu*
Hebron (Labrador)
Before 1912 *Avant 1912*
Ivory *Ivoire*
2.5 x 4.5 x 3.5

84

Walrus *Morse*
Artist unknown *Artiste inconnu*
Eastern Canadian Arctic *Est de l'Arctique canadien*
Before 1900 *Avant 1900*
Ivory *Ivoire*
2 x 6.5 x 2

85

Walrus head *Tête de morse*
Dorset culture *Culture de Dorset*
Igloolik area *Région d'Igloolik*
Ivory *Ivoire*
1.7 x 4.7 x 1.4

86

Walrus head *Tête de morse*
Dorset culture *Culture de Dorset*
Port aux Choix – 2 site, Newfoundland *Port aux Choix – site 2, Terre-Neuve*
Bone *Os*
4.7 x 6.2 x 1.6

87

Musk-ox *Boeuf musqué*
Artist unknown *Artiste inconnu*
Foxe Basin *Bassin Foxe*
Before 1899 *Avant 1899*
Grey Stone *Pierre grise*
3.8 x 7 x 1.5

88

Fish(lure) *Poisson (leurre)*
Thule culture *Culture de Thulé*
Nerdlivitok
Ivory *Ivoire*
2.25 x 8.25 x 1.2

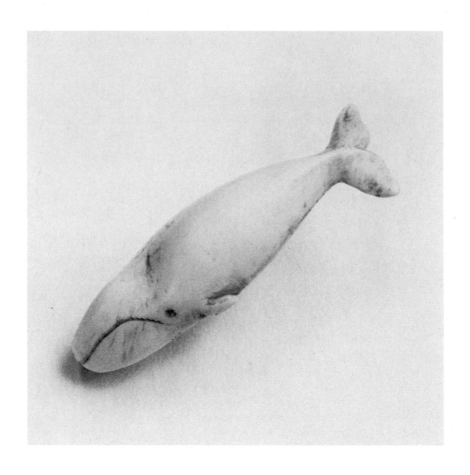

89

Bowhead whale *Baleine Boréale*
Artist unknown *Artiste inconnu*
Eastern Canadian Arctic *Est de l'Arctique canadien*
Before 1900 *Avant 1900*
Ivory *Ivoire*
1 X 3.5 X 1

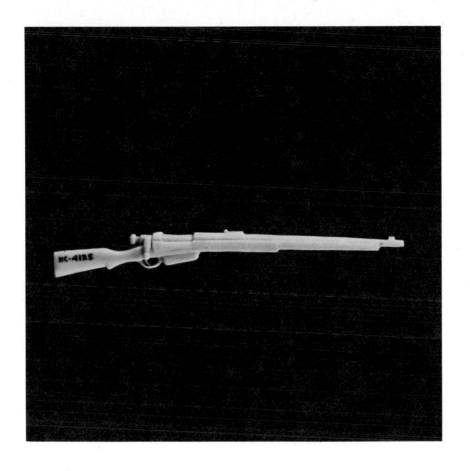

90

Model rifle *Maquette de carabine*
Artist unknown *Artiste inconnu*
Fort Ross
Before 1939 *Avant 1939*
Ivory *Ivoire*
1 x 10.8 x 0.5

91
Man carrying pack *Homme chargé*
Artist unknown *Artiste inconnu*
North Baffin Island *Nord de l'île Baffin*
Before 1930 *Avant 1930*
Ivory *Ivoire*
7 x 3.5 x 3

92 / 93
Standing woman / Man *Femme debout / Homme*
Artist unknown *Artiste inconnu*
East coast of Labrador? *Côte orientale du Labrador?*
Before 1914 *Avant 1914*
Ivory *Ivoire*
2.8 x 1.5 x 1 / 5 x 2.5 x 1

94
Standing hunter with rifle *Chasseur debout avec sa carabine*
Artist unknown *Artiste inconnu*
Eastern Canadian Arctic *Est de l'arctique canadien*
Before 1900 *Avant 1900*
Ivory *Ivoire*
7 x 5.5 x 2

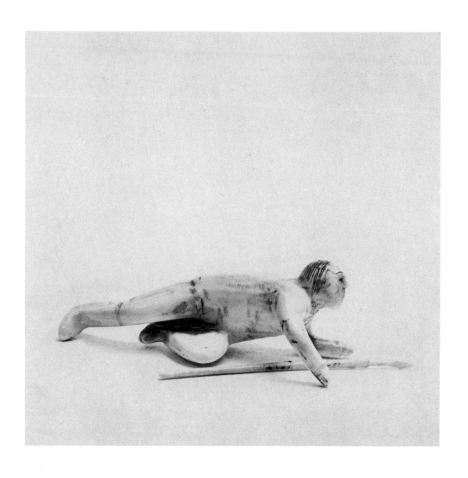

95
Lying hunter with spear *Chasseur étendu avec sa lance*
Artist unknown *Artiste inconnu*
Eastern Canadian Arctic *Est de l'Arctique canadien*
Before 1900 *Avant 1900*
Ivory *Ivoire*
2 x 6.5 x 2

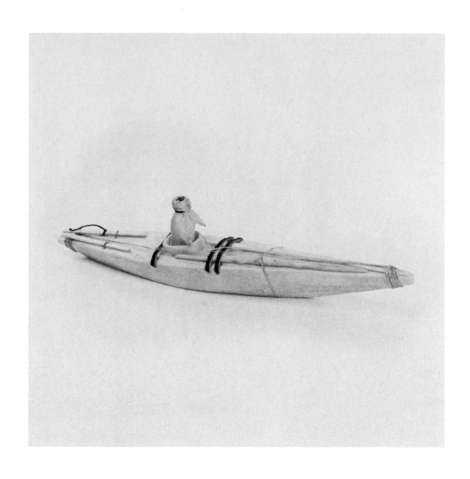

96

Man in kayak *Homme en kayak*
Artist unknown *Artiste inconnu*
East coast of Labrador? *Côte orientale du Labrador?*
Before 1914 *Avant 1914*
Ivory *Ivoire*
3 x 15 x 2.5

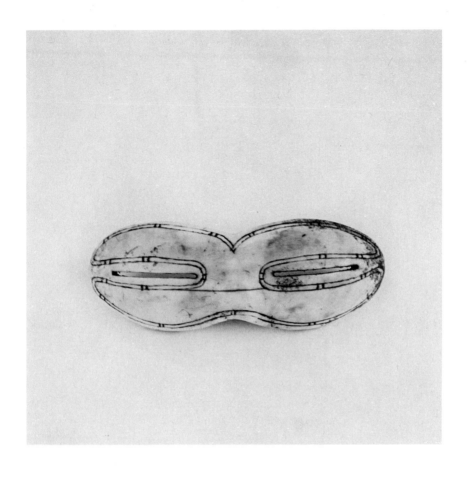

97
Snow goggles *Lunettes contre l'éclat de la neige*
Thule culture *Culture de Thulé*
Maxwell Bay, south of Devon Island *Baie Maxwell sud de l'île Devon*
Ivory *Ivoire*
4 X 11.5 X 1.7

98

Harpoon head *Pointe de harpon*
Thule culture *Culture de Thulé*
Calthorpe Islands *Iles Calthorpe*
Bone *Os*
1.5 x 18.7 x 3.25

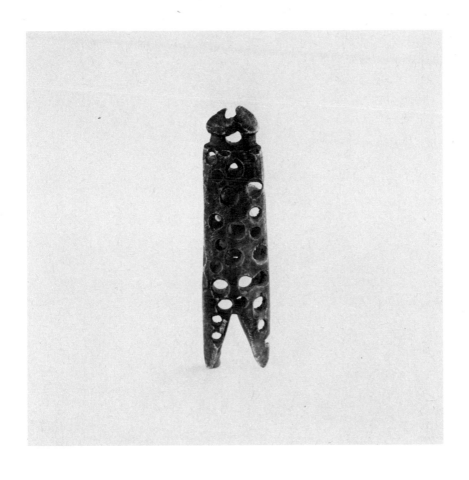

99

Perforated harpoon head *Pointe de harpon perforée*
Thule culture *Culture de Thulé*
Native Point (Southampton Island)
Ivory *Ivoire*
1.5 x 8.3 x 2

100

Model saw *Maquette de scie*
Artist unknown *Artiste inconnu*
Hebron (Labrador)
Before 1912 *Avant 1912*
Ivory *Ivoire*
1.5 x 5.5 x 13

101

Caribou *Caribou*
Anaitok, Augustin 1935–
Pelly Bay
1966
Antler *Andouiller*
12 X 14.5 X 3

102

Man carrying caribou *Homme portant un caribou*
Kavik, John 1897–
Rankin Inlet
1964
Black stone *Pierre noire*
16.5 x 16.5 x 6.3

103

Man carrying young caribou *Homme portant un jeune caribou*
Atok, John 1906–
Eskimo Point
1969
Light grey-green stone and antler *Pierre vert-de-gris clair et andouiller*
12 X 10 X 7

104
Man carrying fox *Homme portant un renard*
Shoovagar 1904–
Cape Dorset
ca. 1955
Dark grey stone *Pierre gris foncé*
17.5 x 11.5 x 6

105

Man holding up two fish *Homme portant deux poissons*
Koodluarlik, Kakasilala 1913–
Pangnirtung
1968
Whale bone *Os de baleine*
16.5 x 20.5 x 12

106

Fisherman carrying his catch *Pêcheur portant sa prise*
Oogark, Fabien 1923–
Pelly Bay
1964
Ivory *Ivoire*
8.5 x 4 x 3

107

Fisherman carrying his catch *Pêcheur portant sa prise*
Apsaktauk, Otto 1935–
Pelly Bay
ca. 1955
Ivory *Ivoire*
5.7 x 3.5 x 2.7

108

Hunter with raised arms *Chasseur aux bras levés*
Ohaytook, Lucassie 1921–
Belcher Islands *Iles Belcher*
1966
Grey-green stone *Pierre vert-de-gris*
12 x 11.5 x 6

109

Head and torso of a bear *Tête et torse d'ours*
Amidilak
Inoucdjouac (Port Harrison)
1953
Black stone and ivory *Pierre noire et ivoire*
17.5 X 11 X 14

110

Head of a walrus *Tête de morse*
Ugjuk, Thomas 1921–
Whale Cove
ca. 1966
Whale bone and ivory *Os de baleine et ivoire*
26 x 41 x 19

III

Caribou *Caribou*
Annanak, George 1904–1968
Port Nouveau-Québec (George River)
1957
Black stone and antler *Pierre noire et andouiller*
24 x 26 x 19

112

Musk-ox *Boeuf musqué*
Tattener, George 1910–
Baker Lake
1963
Dark grey stone and ivory *Pierre gris foncé et ivoire*
14 x 22 x 6

II3
Musk-ox *Boeuf musqué*
Artist unknown *Artiste inconnu*
Igloolik?
ca. 1959
Dark green stone and ivory *Pierre vert foncé et ivoire*
8 x 16 x 4.5

114

Musk-ox *Boeuf musqué*
Kingeelik, James 1912–
Baker Lake
1963
Black stone and horn *Pierre noire et corne*
11.5 x 20 x 6

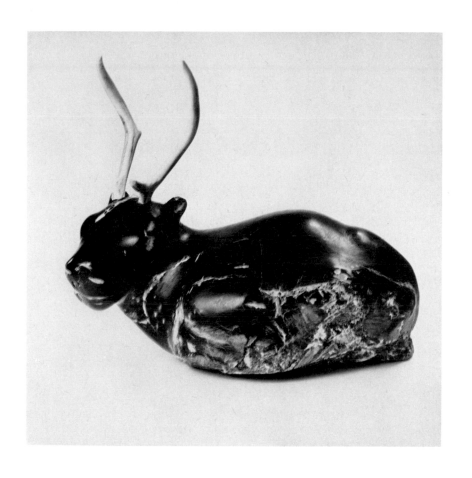

II5

Caribou *Caribou*
Makpa, Vital Arnasungnark 1922–
Baker Lake
1962
Black mottled stone *Pierre marbrée de noir*
28 x 35 x 19

116

Wolf devouring dead caribou *Loup dévorant un caribou mort*
Kulluaijuk, Uili 1946–
Saglouc (Sugluk)
1957
Grey stone *Pierre grise*
10.5 X 31.5 X 12.8

117
Howling dog *Chien hurlant*
Kananginak 1935–
Cape Dorset
1956–57
Dark grey stone *Pierre gris foncé*
31 X 10 X 15

118

Bear protecting her cub *Ourse protégeant son ourson*
Kanagna, Elisapee f 1918–
Arctic Bay
1960
Whale bone *Os de baleine*
14.8 x 6 x 13.5

119

Stalking bear *Ours à l'affût*
Kaunak, John 1941–
Repulse Bay
1963
Grey stone *Pierre grise*
9 x 26 x 7

120

Polar bear *Ours blanc*
Kittosuk, Charlie 1927–
Belcher Islands *Iles Belcher*
1966
Grey-green stone *Pierre vert-de-gris*
17 X 12.5 X 9.5

121

Bear on ice *Ours sur la glace*
Manno 1923–
Cape Dorset
1964
Light grey-green stone *Pierre vert-de-gris clair*
9 x 17 x 8.5

122

Bear family *Famille d'ours*
Pauta 1916–
Cape Dorset
1956–57
Green stone *Pierre verte*
18 x 14 x 11.5

123

Cache of seals *Cache de phoques*
Artist unknown *Artiste inconnu*
Belcher Islands *Iles Belcher*
1955
Grey-green stone *Pierre vert-de-gris*
9.5 × 9 × 7

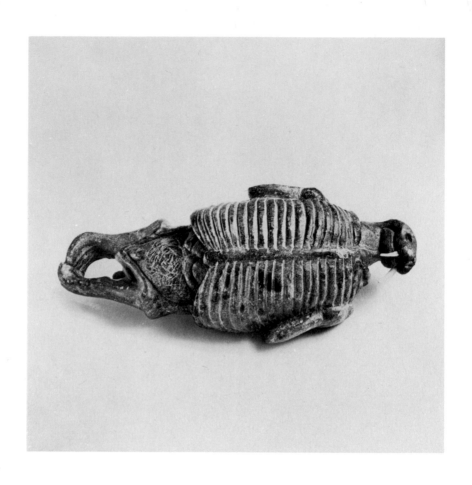

124

Flensed walrus *Morse écorché*
Artist unknown *Artiste inconnu*
Saglouc? (Sugluk?)
1954
Dark green and orange stone *Pierre vert foncé et orange*
6 x 18.5 x 7.5

125
Howling dog *Chien hurlant*
Iyola 1933–
Cape Dorset
1960
Green stone *Pierre verte*
21 X 12 X 9

126

Caribou *Caribou*
Artist unknown *Artiste inconnu*
North Baffin Island *Nord de l'île Baffin*
Before 1930 *Avant 1930*
Ivory *Ivoire*
3.2 x 5 x 1.3

127
Caribou *Caribou*
Artist unknown *Artiste inconnu*
Cape Dorset
Before 1925 *Avant 1925*
Ivory *Ivoire*
5.5 x 8 x 5

128

Young caribou *Jeune caribou*
Sheeookjuk 1920–
Cape Dorset
ca. 1964
Dark green stone *Pierre vert foncé*
15.5 x 17 x 6.5

129
Musk-ox *Boeuf musqué*
Artist unknown *Artiste inconnu*
Eastern Canadian Arctic *Est de l'Arctique canadien*
Before 1900 *Avant 1900*
Ivory and horn *Ivoire et corne*
4.5 X 7.5 X 2

130

Musk-ox *Boeuf musqué*
Artist unknown *Artiste inconnu*
Foxe Basin *Bassin Foxe*
Before 1906 *Avant 1906*
Ivory and horn *Ivoire et corne*
5 x 7.5 x 2.5

131
Musk-ox *Boeuf musqué*
Artist unknown *Artiste inconnu*
Eastern Canadian Arctic *Est de l'Arctique canadien*
Black stone and horn *Pierre noire et corne*
6.5 x 9.5 x 3

132
Musk-ox *Boeuf musqué*
Toolooktook, Paul 1947–
Baker Lake
1964
Dark grey stone *Pierre gris foncé*
17 x 31 x 12

133

Musk-ox *Boeuf musqué*
Tungilik, Mark 1913–
Repulse Bay
ca. 1951
Ivory *Ivoire*
5 x 8 x 3

134

Musk-ox *Boeuf musqué*
Amarook, Michael 1941–
Baker Lake
ca. 1962
Black stone *Pierre noire*
18 x 24 x 13

135

Musk-ox *Boeuf musqué*
Artist unknown *Artiste inconnu*
Foxe Basin *Bassin Foxe*
Before 1902 *Avant 1902*
Horn *Corne*
4.5 x 8 x 1.6

136
Wounded bear *Ours blessé*
Artist unknown *Artiste inconnu*
Povungnituk
1953–54
Grey stone and ivory *Pierre grise et ivoire*
11 X 20 X 13.5

137
Bear on hind legs *Ours dressé sur ses pattes de derrière*
Artist unknown *Artiste inconnu*
Inoucdjouac (Port Harrison)
1954
Green stone *Pierre verte*
21.5 x 7.5 x 11.5

138
Wounded bear *Ours blessé*
Artist unknown *Artiste inconnu*
Inoucdjouac (Port Harrison)
ca. 1954
Black stone *Pierre noire*
12 x 23 x 11.5

139
Caribou *Caribou*
Artist unknown *Artiste inconnu*
Baker Lake
1963
Black stone and bone *Pierre noire et ivoire*
6.5 x 11.5 x 4

140

Two caribou *Deux caribous*
Nassak, Sammy 1905–
Bellin (Payne Bay)
1966
Black stone *Pierre noire*
12 x 18 x 6
7.5 x 17 x 4.5

141

Caribou *Caribou*
Tegodlerrak, Solomonie 1924–
Clyde River
1964
Black stone and wood *Pierre noire et bois*
19 x 31 x 5

142

Musk-ox *Boeuf musqué*
Pauta 1916–
Cape Dorset
1962
Green stone *Pierre verte*
26.5 x 26 x 10.5

143

Kneeling caribou *Caribou agenouillé*
Oshooweetook 'B' 1923–
Cape Dorset
1970
Green stone and bone *Pierre verte et os*
37 x 44 x 29

144
Wolf attacking caribou *Loup attaquant un caribou*
Oogark, Fabien 1923–
Pelly Bay
Before 1965 *Avant 1965*
Ivory *Ivoire*
10 x 28.5 x 2.5

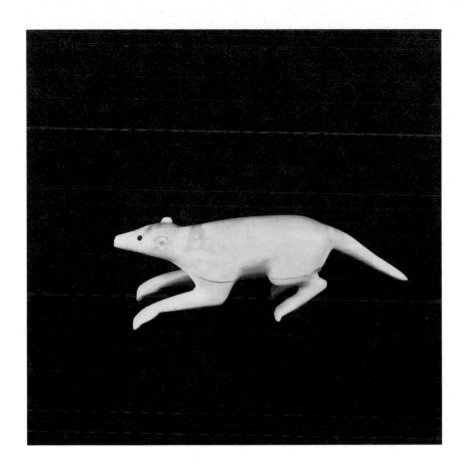

145
Running dog *Chien courant*
Piluardjuk 1901–
Repulse Bay
ca. 1961
Ivory *Ivoire*
4 x 12 x 2.5

146

Kneeling caribou *Caribou agenouillé*
Piluardjuk 1901–
Repulse Bay
1960–62
Ivory *Ivoire*
12 X 14 X 2.5

147

Caribou head *Tête de caribou*
Miki 1918–
Whale Cove
1965–66
Light grey stone and antler *Pierre gris clair et andouiller*
29.5 x 22.5 x 14

148
Seal head *Tête de phoque*
Tavitee
Cape Dorset
Before 1953 *Avant 1953*
Dark green stone and ivory *Pierre vert foncé et ivoire*
8 x 18 x 10

149
Seal *Phoque*
Artist unknown *Artiste inconnu*
West Baffin Island *Ouest de l'île Baffin*
19th century *19e siècle*
Ivory *Ivoire*
5.5 x 11.5 x 2.5

150
Multiple image *Image composée*
Artist unknown *Artiste inconnu*
Eastern Canadian Arctic *Est de l'Arctique canadien*
Before 1914 *Avant 1914*
Bone *Os*
4.5 X 29 X 2.5

151
Multiple image *Image composée*
Artist unknown *Artiste inconnu*
Eastern Canadian Arctic *Est de l'Arctique canadien*
Before 1914 *Avant 1914*
Ivory *Ivoire*
4.5 X 21 X 3

152

Bear on hind legs *Ours dressé sur ses pattes de derrière*
Tudlik 1890–1962
Cape Dorset
1952
Black stone *Pierre noire*
28.5 x 10.5 x 9.5

I53
Bear *Ours*
Artist unknown *Artiste inconnu*
Saglouc (Sugluk)
1949
Bone and ivory *Os et ivoire*
10 x 22 x 6

154
Fish *Poisson*
Aculiak, Joe Adlikit 1936–
Inoucdjouac (Port Harrison)
1958
Dark green stone *Pierre vert foncé*
7.5 x 16 x 5

155
Walrus *Morse*
Simigak 1939–
Cape Dorset
1965
Green stone *Pierre verte*
20 X 39 X 29

156
Owl *Harfang*
Pudlo 1916–
Cape Dorset
1968
Grey-green stone *Pierre vert-de-gris*
30 x 29 x 30

157

Hawk *Buse*
Axangayuk 1937–
Cape Dorset
1968
Green stone *Pierre verte*
42 x 44 x 49

158
Bear *Ours*
Pauta 1916–
Cape Dorset
1964
Black stone and ivory *Pierre noire et ivoire*
43 x 36 x 35

159
Owl *Harfang*
Kablutsiak, Nancy f 1935–
Eskimo Point
Whale bone *Os de baleine*
1969
12.5 X 14 X 13.5

160

Spirit *Esprit*
Artist unknown *Artiste inconnu*
Cape Dorset
1952–53
Black stone and engraved walrus mandible
Pierre noire et mandibule de morse gravée
16 x 21 x 23

161

Composition of tree with owl *Harfang juché sur un arbre*
Kakee, Josephee 1934–
Pangnirtung
1968
Whale bone *Os de baleine*
66 x 81 x 26

162

Bird *Oiseau*
Tattener, George 1910–
Baker Lake
1962
Black stone *Pierre noire*
10 x 22 x 18

163
Owl *Harfang*
Makpa, Vital Arnakingook 1922–
Baker Lake
1962
Black stone *Pierre noire*
20 x 20 x 11.5

164
Owl *Harfang*
Artist unknown *Artiste inconnu*
Povungnituk
1957
Black stone *Pierre noire*
15.5 x 16 x 23

165
Hawk *Buse*
Oshooweetook 'B' 1923–
Cape Dorset
1966–67
Green stone *Pierre verte*
42 x 27 x 5.5

166

Hawk on one leg *Buse sur une patte*
Oshooweetook 'B' 1923–
Cape Dorset
1968
Green stone *Pierre verte*
49 X 41 X 12

167
Owl *Harfang*
Kataq, Irene f 1914–1971
Repulse Bay
1959
Whale bone *Os de baleine*
16.5 x 11.5 x 10.5

168

Owl with fish in beak *Harfang tenant un poisson dans son bec*
Oshooweetook 'B' 1923–
Cape Dorset
1964
Dark green stone *Pierre vert foncé*
17 x 16 x 8

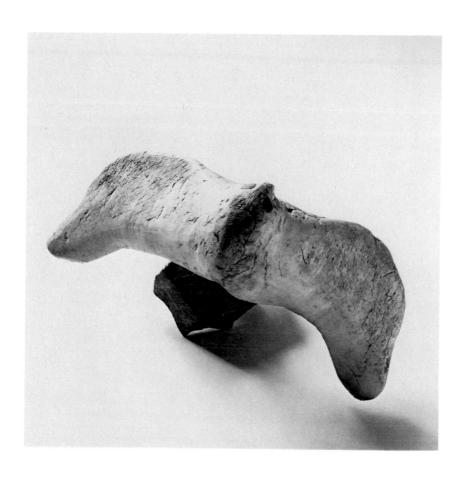

169

Flying bird *Oiseau en vol*
Nootaraloo, Elizabeth f 1914–
Eskimo Point
1969
Whale bone *Os de baleine*
12 x 21 x 8.5

170
Owl *Harfang*
Artist unknown *Artiste inconnu*
Inoucdjouac (Port Harrison)
1951–52
Black stone *Pierre noire*
18 x 31 x 7

171
Owl *Harfang*
Eeleeseepee f 1927–
Cape Dorset
1968–69
Green stone *Pierre verte*
15 X 31 X 20

172

Owl alighting *Harfang se posant*
Pudlo 1916–
Cape Dorset
1968
Green mottled stone *Pierre marbrée de vert*
32 x 22 x 14

173
Bird *Oiseau*
Moses 1924–
Inoucdjouac (Port Harrison)
1957
Black stone *Pierre noire*
5 x 7 x 7.5

174
Owl *Harfang*
Qirluaq 1950–
Repulse Bay
ca. 1968
Grey-green mottled stone *Pierre marbrée de vert-de-gris*
15.5 x 12.5 x 7.5

175
Bird *Oiseau*
Elijassiapik 1912–
Inoucdjouac (Port Harrison)
1959
Dark green stone and ivory *Pierre vert foncé et ivoire*
22 X 12 X 9

176

Bird alighting *Oiseau se posant*
Artist unknown *Artiste inconnu*
Cape Dorset
1958–59
Black stone *Pierre noire*
17 X 16 X 21

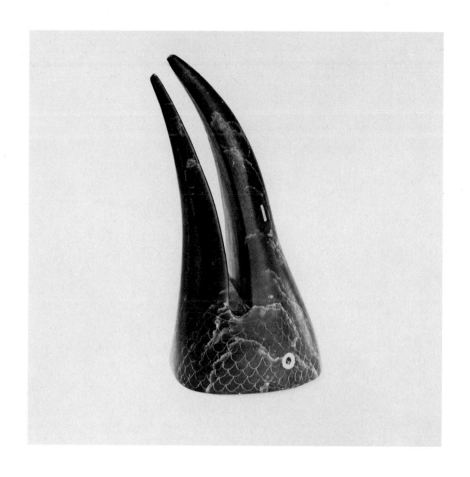

177
Head of a bird *Tête d'oiseau*
Amidilak
Inoucdjouac (Port Harrison)
1954
Dark green stone *Pierre vert foncé*
18 x 10.5 x 6.5

178
Hawk *Buse*
Artist unknown *Artiste inconnu*
Cape Dorset
ca. 1968
Green and black stone *Pierre verte et noire*
5.5 x 5 x 3.2

179
Bird with wings spread *Oiseau aux ailes étendues*
Sheeookjuk 1920–
Cape Dorset
ca. 1960
Green stone *Pierre verte*
12 X 24 X 5

180

Bird *Oiseau*
Igaiju, Aisapik 'Pov' 1915–
Povungnituk
1962
Black stone *Pierre noire*
10.5 x 16 x 7

181

Two loons *Deux huarts*
Artist unknown *Artiste inconnu*
Povungnituk
ca. 1955
Dark grey stone *Pierre gris foncé*
7 x 16 x 17

182

Loon swimming *Huart nageant*
Artist unknown *Artiste inconnu*
Inoucdjouac (Port Harrison)
1956
Black stone *Pierre noire*
6.5 x 21 x 6

183

Sea pigeon *Pigeon de mer*
Niviaxie, Cornelius 1940–
Inoucdjouac (Port Harrison)
1954–55
Dark green stone *Pierre vert foncé*
4.5 x 20 x 8.5

184
Owl *Harfang*
Oopik f 1946–
Cape Dorset
1968
Grey stone *Pierre grise*
13.5 x 22 x 8

185
Owl *Harfang*
Artist unknown *Artiste inconnu*
Inoucdjouac (Port Harrison)
1952–53
Black stone *Pierre noire*
21 x 36 x 9

186

Owl *Harfang*
Kiakshuk 1886–1966
Cape Dorset
1960
Whale bone *Os de baleine*
13 x 12 x 8

187

Sea bird *Oiseau de mer*
Shimout, Joseph 1913–1969
Coral Harbour
1967
Whale bone *Os de baleine*
12 X 22 X 17

188

Owl *Harfang*
Kiakshuk 1886–1966
Cape Dorset
1960
Whale bone *Os de baleine*
8 x 7 x 5

189
Owl *Harfang*
Latcholassie 1919–
Cape Dorset
1967
Grey stone *Pierre grise*
24 X 15 X 20

190
Owl *Harfang*
Oshooweetook 'B' 1923–
Cape Dorset
1964
Green stone *Pierre verte*
19 x 17 x 8.5

191

Owl and lemming *Harfang et lemming*
Irkok Jacob 1937–
Eskimo Point
1967
Whale bone and grey stone *Os de baleine et pierre grise*
13 X 17 X 7

192

Owl Man *Homme hibou*
Latcholassie 1919–
Cape Dorset
1962
Green stone *Pierre verte*
17.5 x 12.5 x 15

193

Owl Man *Homme hibou*
Latcholassie 1919–
Cape Dorset
1960
Green stone *Pierre verte*
23 x 17.5 x 6

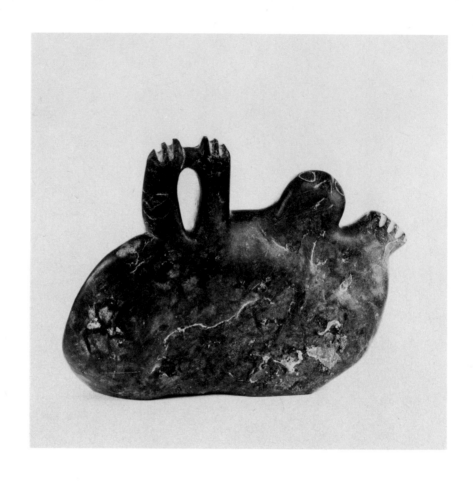

194
Bird *Oiseau*
Latcholassie 1919–
Cape Dorset
1968
Dark green stone *Pierre vert foncé*
24 X 33 X 7

195

Bird Mother *Mère d'oiseau*
Eeteeguyakjuak f 1923–
Cape Dorset
1968
Grey and orange stone *Pierre grise et orange*
27 x 23 x 10

196

Group of five owls *Groupe de cinq harfangs*
Tudlik 1890–1962
Cape Dorset
ca. 1957
Green stone *Pierre verte*
6.5 x 10 x 5
6 x 8 x 4
8 x 4.5 x 4.5
8 x 6.5 x 5
9.5 x 7 x 6

197

Ptarmigans *Lagopèdes*
Joanassie 1935–
Cape Dorset
1960
Black stone *Pierre noire*
6 x 5 x 3
6.5 x 5 x 3
7 x 6 x 4
3.5 x 4 x 2.5
4.5 x 4.5 x 1.8

198

Owl *Harfang*
Lukta 1928–
Cape Dorset
1960
Green stone *Pierre verte*
10 X 11.5 X 7.5

199
Double owl *Harfang double*
Tudlik 1890–1962
Cape Dorset
1960–61
Green stone *Pierre verte*
11 X 10 X 7

200

Owl and seagull *Harfang et goéland*
Echalook, Levi 1918–
Inoucdjouac (Port Harrison)
1954
Black stone *Pierre noire*
16.5 x 18 x 6.5

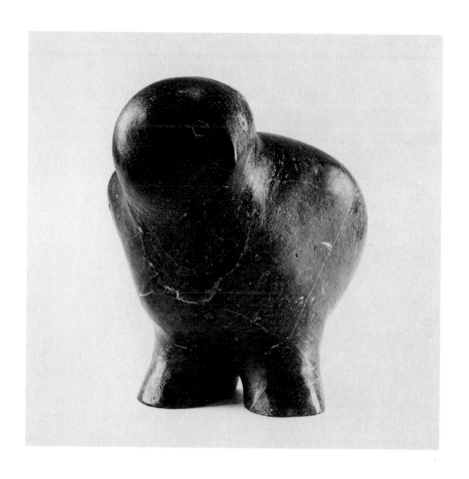

201
Owl *Harfang*
Neooktook, Irenee 1937–
Baker Lake
1963
Black stone *Pierre noire*
20 X 17.5 X 21

202

Owls *Harfangs*
Munnurme 'A' 1917–
Cape Dorset
1967
Green stone *Pierre verte*
31 x 24 x 12

203
Owl *Harfang*
Axangayuk 1937–
Cape Dorset
1964
Green stone *Pierre verte*
5.5 x 16 x 7

204

Owl *Harfang*
Tudlik 1890–1962
Cape Dorset
1960
Green stone *Pierre verte*
9 x 17 x 4.5

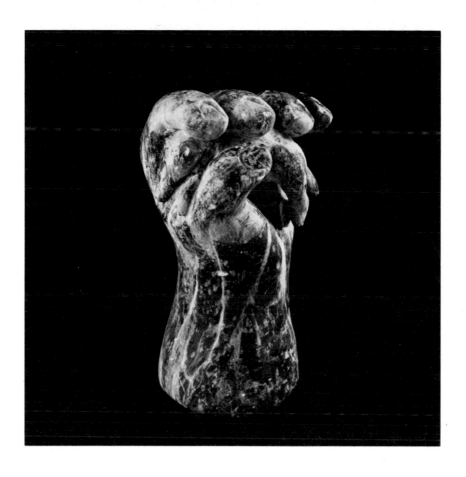

205
Hand holding husky pup *Main tenant un chiot Husky*
Epirk 1923
Arctic Bay
ca. 1967
Green stone *Pierre verte*
15 x 8.5 x 7.5

206

Bust of a crowned figure *Buste d'un personnage couronné*
Artist unknown *Artiste inconnu*
Cape Dorset
1956
Dark grey-green stone *Pierre vert-de-gris foncé*
9 x 8.5 x 4

207

Bust of a crowned figure *Buste d'un personnage couronné*
Artist unknown *Artiste inconnu*
Cape Dorset
1956
Grey stone *Pierre grise*
10.5 X 9 X 4.5

208

Woman with large hood *Femme coiffée d'un grand capuchon*
Artist unknown *Artiste inconnu*
Saglouc? (Sugluk?)
1954
Light green stone *Pierre vert clair*
16.5 x 6 x 4.5

209

Woman *Femme*
Kittosuk, Caroline f 1911–
Belcher Islands *Iles Belcher*
1950–55
Grey-green stone *Pierre vert-de-gris*
14.5 x 7 x 4

2 I 0

Standing woman *Femme debout*
Artist unknown *Artiste inconnu*
Lake Harbour
1956
Green stone *Pierre verte*
17.5 x 8.5 x 5.5

211

Woman *Femme*
Artist unknown *Artiste inconnu*
Inoucdjouac (Port Harrison)
1949
Ochre stone *Pierre ocre*
9 X 5.5 X 2

212
Box with animal heads and human face
Boîte décorée de têtes d'animaux et d'un visage
Artist unknown *Artiste inconnu*
Povungnituk or *ou* Inoucdjouac (Port Harrison)
1950
Black, grey and ochre stone *Pierre noire, grise et ocre*
5.3 x 10.5 x 4.5

213
Eskimo recollection *Réminiscence esquimaude*
Artist unknown *Artiste inconnu*
Inoucdjouac (Port Harrison)
1951
Ochre and grey stone *Pierre ocre et grise*
2 X 12 X 12

214

Bust of man holding mask *Buste d'un homme tenant un masque à la main*
Kowcharlie deceased *décédé*
Belcher Islands *Iles Belcher*
1954
Dark green and orange stone and ivory *Pierre vert foncé et orange, et ivoire*
8.5 x 16 x 7

215
The migration *La migration*
Talirunili, Joe 1899–
Povungnituk
1964
Grey stone, bone and skin *Pierre grise, os et peau*
33 x 32 x 19

216
Man in sleeping bag *Homme dans un sac de couchage*
Mamgark, Andrew 1930–
Eskimo Point
1967
Grey stone *Pierre grise*
6.5 x 17 x 10

217

Sculpin *Chabot du nord*
Artist unknown *Artiste inconnu*
Saglouc (Sugluk)
1957
Grey-green stone *Pierre vert-de-gris*
9 x 25.5 x 11.5

218

Two sleeping families *Deux familles endormies*
Sheeookjuk 1920–
Cape Dorset
1953
Grey stone and ivory *Pierre grise et ivoire*
5 x 16 x 16

219

Drum dancer *Danseur au son du tambour*
Ahlooloo, Peter 1908–
Arctic Bay
1962
Whale bone and various *Os de baleine et autres*
14.5 X 12.5 X 9

220

Drum dancer *Danseur au son du tambour*
Issirkrut, Madeleine f 1928–
Repulse Bay
1962
Grey stone and bone *Pierre grise et os*
16.5 x 6 x 16.5

221

Drum dancer *Danseur au son du tambour*
Artist unknown *Artiste inconnu*
Coppermine
Before 1920 *Avant 1920*
Black stone and various *Pierre noire et autres*
13 x 8 x 11

222

Drum dancer *Danseur au son du tambour*
Iguptaq, Bernadette f 1931–
Repulse Bay
1963–64
Grey stone and bone *Pierre grise et os*
9.5 x 5 x 13.5

223

Somersaulting man *Homme exécutant une pirouette*
Kavik, John 1897–
Rankin Inlet
1964
Black stone *Pierre noire*
15 x 8 x 3

224
Kneeling boy *Garçon agenouillé*
Konak
Inoucdjouac (Port Harrison)
1953
Ochre stone *Pierre ocre*
6 x 3 x 3.5

225
Man with fiddle *Homme avec violon*
Artist unknown *Artiste inconnu*
Bellin (Payne Bay)
1953
Grey stone *Pierre grise*
3.5 × 7 × 4

226
Singing psalms *Le chant des psaumes*
Polik, John 1901–
Eskimo Point
1966
Bone *Os*
6.3 x 10.8 x 6.3

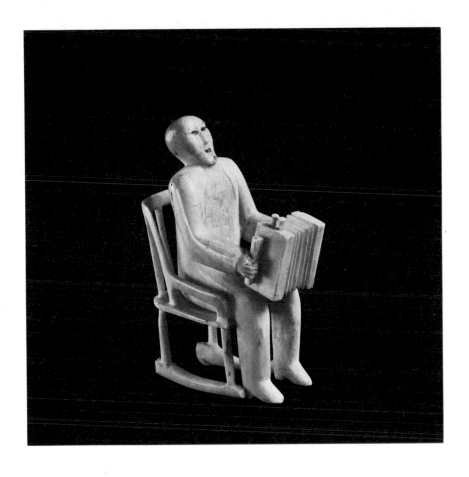

227

Man in rocking chair playing concertina
Homme assis sur une berceuse et jouant de l'accordéon
Artist unknown *Artiste inconnu*
Northern Baffin Island *Nord de l'île Baffin*
1929–31
Ivory *Ivoire*
9 x 3 x 5.5

228

Acrobatics on a rope in an igloo *Acrobaties sur un câble dans un igloo*
Nugyugalik, Moses 1910–
Baker Lake
1968
Bone *Os*
21 X 19 X 12

229

Man chanting *Homme psalmodiant*
Koodluarlik, Kakasilala 1913–
Pangnirtung
1968
Whale bone *Os de baleine*
15 x 9 x 5

230
Seal hunter *Chasseur de phoques*
Saggiak 1897–
Cape Dorset
1952
Whale bone *Os de baleine*
4 x 7 x 8

231

Kneeling man and dog *Homme agenouillé et chien*
Attributed to *Attribué à* Tudlik 1890–1962
Cape Dorset
ca. 1956
Dark grey-green stone *Pierre vert-de gris foncé*
13 x 13 x 7.5

232

Hunter at seal hole *Chasseur à un trou de phoques*
Artist unknown *Artiste inconnu*
Povungnituk
1948
Dark grey stone *Pierre gris foncé*
17 X 9 X 7

233

Igloo (model) *Igloo (maquette)*
Artists unknown *Artistes inconnus*
Aivilik
Before 1899 *Avant 1899*
Grey stone *Pierre grise*
4 x 4 x 10.5
6 x 8 x 7
4 x 7 x 8
3 x 8 x 8

234
Mother and two children *Mère et deux enfants*
Artist unknown *Artiste inconnu*
Repulse Bay
1963–64
Ivory *Ivoire*
8 x 3.8 x 3.8

235
Standing man *Homme debout*
Willie
Inoucdjouac (Port Harrison)
ca. 1958
Dark grey stone and bone *Pierre gris foncé et os*
16 x 23.5 x 10

236
Mother and child *Mère et enfant*
Tasseor, Lucy f 1934–
Eskimo Point
1968
Black stone *Pierre noire*
4.5 X 2 X 2

237
Woman with pot on lap *Femme avec un pot sur les genoux*
Kopinar, Monique f 1913–
Eskimo Point
1967
Grey-green stone *Pierre vert-de-gris*
19 X 16.5 X 7

238
Nude female figure *Femme nue*
Ikkuma, Bernard 1912–
Igloolik
1967
Dark grey stone *Pierre gris foncé*
10.5 x 4 x 2.5

239
Man eating fish *Homme mangeant un poisson*
Ahlooloo, Peter 1908–
Arctic Bay
1962
Whale bone and ivory *Os de baleine et ivoire*
10 X 11 X 15.5

240
Mother and child with ulu *Mère et enfant avec un ulu*
Elizabeth f –1950
Inoucdjouac (Port Harrison)
1950
Black stone *Pierre noire*
6.5 x 3 x 3

241
Woman pulling intestines from a goose *Femme évident d'une oie*
Eli –1958
Inoucdjouac (Port Harrison)
1953
Dark green and orange stone *Pierre vert foncé et orange*
12.5 x 14 x 10.5

242

Woman holding ulu *Femme tenant un ulu*
Axangayuk 1937–
Cape Dorset
ca. 1966
Green stone *Pierre verte*
32 x 23 x 15

243
Woman with bowl *Femme avec bol*
Tiktak 1916–
Rankin Inlet
1963
Black stone *Pierre noire*
18 x 13 x 17

244
Woman with ulu and fish *Femme avec ulu et poisson*
Nuktialuk, Pinnie 1934–1969
Inoucdjouac (Port Harrison)
1954
Dark green stone and ivory *Pierre vert foncé et ivoire*
11 X 22 X 14

245

Mother with hatchet *Mère avec hachette*
Kagvik, Davidee 1915–
Poste-de-la-Baleine (Great Whale River)
1967
Grey-green stone *Pierre vert-de-gris*
27 X 21 X 17

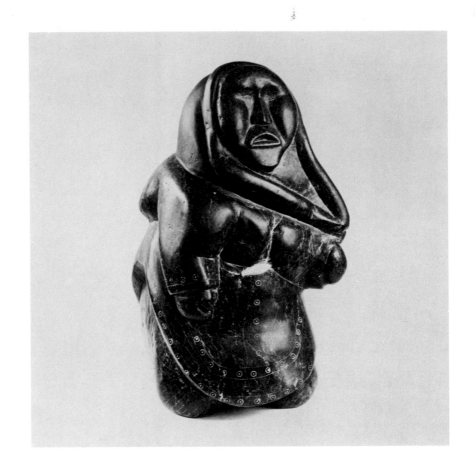

246
Old woman *Femme âgée*
Weetaltuk, Saroli 1906–1964
Inoucdjouac (Port Harrison)
1957
Black stone and ivory *Pierre noire et ivoire*
48 x 27 x 33.5

247
Woman in childbirth *Femme accouchant*
Erkoolik, Toona 1935–
Baker Lake
1963
Black stone *Pierre noire*
31.5 x 24.5 x 21.5

248
Family *Famille*
Makpa, Vital Arnasungnark 1922–
Baker Lake
1963
Black stone *Pierre noire*
31 X 33 X 29

249
Mother and child *Mère et enfant*
Artist unknown *Artiste inconnu*
Poste-de-la-Baleine (Great Whale River)
ca. 1964
Grey-green stone *Pierre vert-de-gris*
15 x 16 x 16

2 50

Woman on a base *Femme sur sole*
Artist unknown *Artiste inconnu*
Inoucdjouac (Port Harrison)
1949
Dark grey stone *Pierre gris foncé*
17 x 12 x 6

251

Woman holding three puppies *Femme tenant trois chiots*
Kooparpik 1931–
Cape Dorset
1961–62
Green stone *Pierre verte*
25 x 16 x 20

252
Woman holding seal *Femme tenant un phoque*
Niviaksiak 1908–1959
Cape Dorset
1958
Green stone *Pierre verte*
32 x 17 x 24

253
Mother and child *Mère et enfant*
attributed to *attribué à* Mummookshoarluk, Victoria f 1930–
Baker Lake
ca. 1964
Black stone *Pierre noire*
36 x 21 x 13

254

Mother and child *Mère et enfant*
Tartuk, Felicité f 1924–
Repulse Bay
1964–65
Light grey stone *Pierre gris clair*
10.5 x 8 x 7

2 5 5
Mother and child *Mère et enfant*
Polik, John 1901–
Eskimo Point
1967
Black stone *Pierre noire*
14 x 18.5 x 11

256
Mother holding child *Mère tenant un enfant*
Katoo, Madeleine f 1916–
Eskimo Point
1967
Grey stone *Pierre grise*
13 x 8.5 x 4

257

Mother and child *Mère et enfant*
Kowjakalook 1906–
Lake Harbour
1961
Ochre stone *Pierre ocre*
12 X 5 X 5

258
Group of three *Groupe de trois*
Pangnark, John 1920–
Eskimo Point
1968
Black stone *Pierre noire*
12.5 x 14.5 x 14.5

259
Mother and child *Mère et enfant*
Kallooar, Francis 1931–
Baker Lake
1963–64
Black stone *Pierre noire*
19 X 13.5 X 11

260

Mother and child with fish *Mère et enfant avec un poisson*
Artist unknown *Artiste inconnu*
Inoucdjouac (Port Harrison)
ca. 1953
Dark green and orange stone and ivory *Pierre vert foncé et orange, et ivoire*
26 x 20 x 26

261

Mother and child *Mère et enfant*
Artist unknown *Artiste inconnu*
Inoucdjouac (Port Harrison)
1952–53
Green stone *Pierre verte*
15 x 15 x 19

262

Father and child *Père et enfant*
Ekoota, David 1929–
Baker Lake
1963
Black stone *Pierre noire*
21 x 30 x 14

263
Mother and child *Mère et enfant*
Ekoota, David 1929–
Baker Lake
1965
Greenish-black stone *Pierre noire verdâtre*
31 X 13.5 X 9

264
Mother and child *Mère et enfant*
Artist unknown *Artiste inconnu*
Saglouc? (Sugluk?)
1952–53
Dark grey stone *Pierre gris foncé*
36 x 32 x 16

265
Mother and child *Mère et enfant*
Angnako, Josephee 1900–1966
Pangnirtung
1955–56
Black stone and ivory *Pierre noire et ivoire*
33 x 13.5 x 8

266
Mother fishing *Mère pêchant*
Uyaoperk, Margaret f 1905–
Eskimo Point
1967
Dark grey stone *Pierre gris foncé*
25 x 26 x 18

267

Mother and child with basket *Mère et enfant avec un panier*
Artist unknown *Artiste inconnu*
Inoucdjouac (Port Harrison)
1952
Dark grey stone and ivory *Pierre gris foncé et ivoire*
24 X 17 X 15

268
Mother and child *Mère et enfant*
Artist unknown *Artiste inconnu*
Inoucdjouac (Port Harrison)
ca. 1956
Black stone *Pierre noire*
15.5 x 18.5 x 17.5

269

Mother nursing child *Mère allaitant son enfant*
Inukpuk, Johnnie 1911–
Inoucdjouac (Port Harrison)
1954
Dark green stone *Pierre vert foncé*
27 X 21 X 23

270
Kneeling mother and child *Mère agenouillée et enfant*
Kogalik
Povungnituk
ca. 1955
Black stone *Pierre noire*
19 X 13.5 X 11

271

Mother and child *Mère et enfant*
Artist unknown *Artiste inconnu*
Inoucdjouac (Port Harrison)
1957
Black stone and sealskin *Pierre noire et peau de phoque*
31 X 21 X 19

272
Mother and child *Mère et enfant*
Artist unknown *Artiste inconnu*
Inoucdjouac (Port Harrison)
1953
Grey stone *Pierre grise*
18 x 42 x 26

273
Mother and child *Mère et enfant*
Artist unknown *Artiste inconnu*
Region unknown *Région inconnue*
ca. 1966
Black stone *Pierre noire*
36 x 16.5 x 18

274
Mother and child *Mère et enfant*
Yassic
Pangnirtung
1969
Whale bone *Os de baleine*
8 x 8 x 8

275

Mother and child *Mère et enfant*
Arnayuinnar, Thomas 1931–
Eskimo Point
1968–69
Whale bone *Os de baleine*
13.5 x 4 x 7.5

276

Mother and child *Mère et enfant*
Artist unknown *Artiste inconnu*
Inoucdjouac (Port Harrison)
1954
Dark green and orange stone *Pierre vert foncé et orange*
19 x 13 x 6

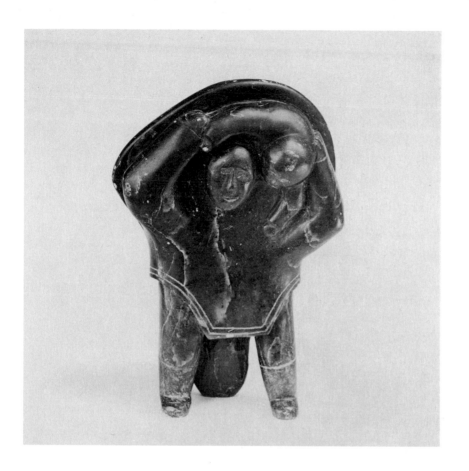

277
Mother and child *Mère et enfant*
Artist unknown *Artiste inconnu*
Inoucdjouac (Port Harrison)
1953
Dark green stone *Pierre vert foncé*
18 x 12 x 9

278
Mother and child *Mère et enfant*
Syollie
Inoucdjouac (Port Harrison)
1957
Dark green stone and ivory *Pierre vert foncé et ivoire*
25 X 20 X 10

279
Mother and child *Mère et enfant*
Artist unknown *Artiste inconnu*
Inoucdjouac (Port Harrison)
1955
Dark green stone *Pierre vert foncé*
19 x 32 x 30

280
Mother and two children *Mère et deux enfants*
Niviaxie, Annie f 1930–
Poste-de-la-Baleine (Great Whale River)
1966
Black stone *Pierre noire*
26 x 10 x 15.5

281

Mother and child *Mère et enfant*
Tiktak 1916–
Rankin Inlet
1966
Dark grey stone *Pierre gris foncé*
48 x 12 x 21

282

Couple *Couple*
Ahlooloo, Peter 1908–
Arctic Bay
1961
Whale bone *Os de baleine*
15 x 15 x 10.5

283
Mother with two children *Mère avec deux enfants*
Pissuyui, Martine f 1933–
Eskimo Point
1967
Dark grey stone *Pierre gris foncé*
23 x 25 x 10

284

Pregnant mother and child *Mère enceinte et enfant*
Kavik, John 1897–
Rankin Inlet
1964
Black stone *Pierre noire*
15 x 6.5 x 5

285
Mother playing with child *Mère jouant avec un enfant*
Kavik, Johnassie 1916–
Belcher Islands *Iles Belcher*
1964
Dark grey stone *Pierre gris foncé*
9 X 17 X 13

286
Mother and child *Mère et enfant*
Tasseor, Lucy f 1934–
Eskimo Point
1969
Black stone *Pierre noire*
10 x 7 x 8

287

Mother and child *Mère et enfant*
Pov, Abraham 1927–
Inoucdjouac (Port Harrison)
ca. 1959
Black stone *Pierre noire*
18 x 16 x 8.5

288

Mother nursing child *Mère allaitant son enfant*
Atok, John 1906–
Eskimo Point
1967
Black stone *Pierre noire*
20 x 19 x 13.5

289

Mother and child *Mère et enfant*
Padlayat, Isaacie Qurquq 1934–
Saglouc (Sugluk)
1956
Dark grey stone *Pierre gris foncé*
19 X 19 X 21

290

Mother with two children *Mère avec deux enfants*
Ekoota, David 1929–
Baker Lake
ca. 1962
Dark grey stone *Pierre gris foncé*
24 x 16.5 x 10

291

Mother and child *Mère et enfant*
Kavik, John 1897–
Rankin Inlet
1968
Dark grey stone *Pierre gris foncé*
17 x 10.5 x 6.5

292
Mother and child *Mère et enfant*
Akeeaktashuk 1898–1954
Inoucdjouac (Port Harrison)
1953
Dark green stone and bone *Pierre vert foncé et os*
11 x 6.5 x 6.5

293

Mother and child with ulu and fish *Mère et enfant avec un ulu et un poisson*
Artist unknown *Artiste inconnu*
Inoucdjouac (Port Harrison)
1954–55
Green stone and ivory *Pierre verte et ivoire*
17 X 11 X 8

294

Mother and child *Mère et enfant*
Utuyak, Eulalie f 1935–
Eskimo Point
1966
Dark grey stone *Pierre gris foncé*
10 x 8 x 11

295

Mother and child *Mère et enfant*
Kakagon, Bessie f 1914–1958
Coppermine
1955
Dark green stone *Pierre vert foncé*
10 x 6.5 x 4

296
Mother and child *Mère et enfant*
Suetakak f 1933–
Eskimo Point
1968
Grey stone *Pierre grise*
15.5 x 13.5 x 7

297
Mother and child *Mère et enfant*
Nanook, Elizabeth f 1910–
Rankin Inlet
1963
Dark grey stone *Pierre gris foncé*
19 X 7 X 7

298
Mother holding child *Mère tenant un enfant*
Koperqualook
Povungnituk
ca. 1954
Dark grey-green stone and ivory *Pierre vert-de-gris foncé et ivoire*
33 X 17 X 25

299

Seated woman *Femme assise*
Mannuk, Johnassie 1929–
Belcher Islands *Iles Belcher*
1964–65
Grey-green stone *Pierre vert-de-gris*
13.5 x 14.5 x 14.5

300
Father and son *Père et fils*
Akeeaktashuk 1898–1954
Inoucdjouac (Port Harrison)
1954
Dark grey stone *Pierre gris foncé*
25 x 26 x 21

301

Family with dog *Famille avec un chien*
Kenojuak f 1927–
Cape Dorset
1968–69
Green stone *Pierre verte*
37 x 35 x 35

302
Mother and child *Mère et enfant*
Akeeah, Matthew 1940–
Baker Lake
1967
Black stone *Pierre noire*
42 x 30 x 21

303
Mother and two children *Mère et deux enfants*
Akeeah, Matthew 1940–
Baker Lake
1965
Black stone *Pierre noire*
31 X 25 X 21

304
Medicine woman *Sorcière*
Kaka 1928–
Cape Dorset
1953
Dark green stone and ivory *Pierre vert foncé et ivoire*
16.5 x 21.5 x 8.5

305

Female figure *Personnage féminin*
Issirkrut, Madeleine f 1928–
Repulse Bay
ca. 1968
Ivory *Ivoire*
1.8 x 4.4 x 1.7

306

Spirit *Esprit*
Natsiapik, Koveyook 1909–
Broughton Island *Ile Broughton*
ca. 1967
Light grey-green stone *Pierre vert-de-gris clair*
24 x 9 x 8

307

Human and bear spirits *Esprits d'un homme et d'un ours*
Jonanassi
Bellin (Payne Bay)
1963
Grey stone *Pierre grise*
13 x 6 x 9

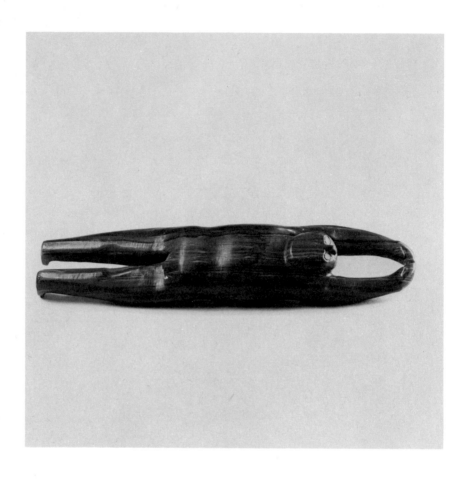

308
Stretched-out man *Homme étendu*
Pukka f 1909–
Arctic Bay
1969
Blue-grey and orange stone *Pierre gris bleu et orange*
6 x 39 x 8.5

309
Merman *Triton*
Kovinaktilliak 'C' 1942–
Cape Dorset
1966
Dark green stone *Pierre vert foncé*
17 X 21 X 11

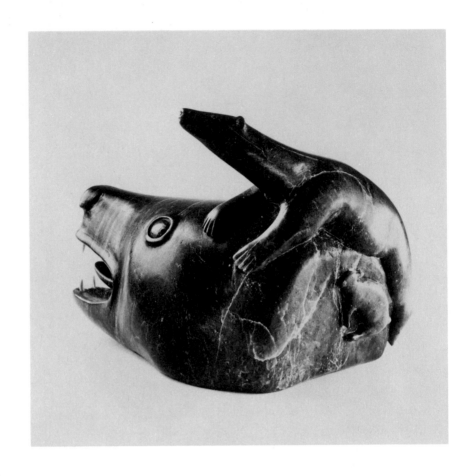

310

Bear head with bear and rabbit *Tête d'ours avec un ours et un lapin*
Audla 1920–
Cape Dorset
1965
Green stone *Pierre verte*
18 x 28 x 18

311
Spirit *Esprit*
Saggiak 1897–
Cape Dorset
1963
Green stone *Pierre verte*
12 x 36 x 17.5

312
Aurora Borealis *Aurore boréale*
Amittu, Davidialu Alasua (Davidealuk) 1910–
Povungnituk
1964
Black stone *Pierre noire*
12.5 x 18 x 5

313

Whale woman *Femme baleine*
Kunuk, Letia f 1923–
Repulse Bay
1968
Grey-green stone *Pierre vert-de-gris*
7.5 x 15.5 x 5

3I4
Sea Man *Triton*
Ekidlak, Paulassie 1934–
Belcher Islands *Iles Belcher*
1968
Grey-green stone *Pierre vert-de-gris*
9 x 29 x 6

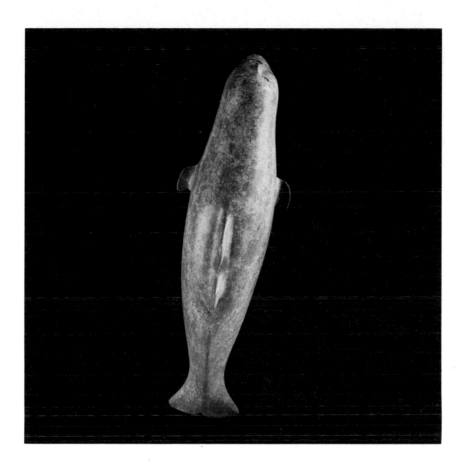

315
Sea spirit (Sedna) *Esprit marin*
Koughajuke 1899–
Lake Harbour
1966
Green stone *Pierre verte*
9 x 34 x 10

316
Bird spirit *Esprit d'oiseau*
Hagiolok, Doris f 1929–
Coppermine
1966
Light grey-green stone *Pierre vert-de-gris clair*
7 x 9.5 x 3.7

317
Sea goddess *Déesse de la mer*
Eliassiepik 1913–196?
Povungnituk
1959
Black stone *Pierre noire*
11 x 22 x 9.5

318

Fish pulling man *Poisson tirant un homme*
Amittu, Davidialu Alasua (Davidealuk) 1910–
Povungnituk
1960
Dark green stone *Pierre vert foncé*
5.5 x 14 x 6.5

319

Sea goddess *Déesse de la mer*
Latcholassie 1919–
Cape Dorset
1963
Green stone *Pierre verte*
12.5 x 28 x 8

320
Good spirit *Bon esprit*
Manaipik, Manasie 1944–
Pangnirtung
1969
Whale bone *Os de baleine*
32 x 48 x 19

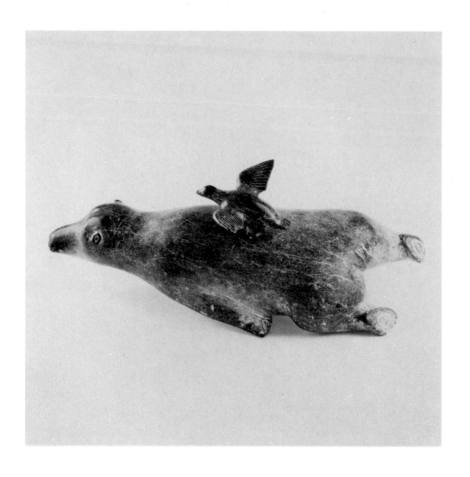

321

Bear with bird on back *Ours avec un oiseau sur son dos*
Artist unknown *Artiste inconnu*
Saglouc (Sugluk)
ca. 1963
Grey stone *Pierre grise*
10.5 x 31 x 10.5

322

Parka image *Sculpture en forme d'anorak*
Kavik, John 1897–
Rankin Inlet
1965
Black stone *Pierre noire*
9.5 x 8.5 x 2

3²3

Spirit *Esprit*
Tunilik, Samuellie 1918–
Cape Dorset
1960
Greenish-black stone *Pierre noire verdâtre*
8 x 4 x 7

3²4
Woman's head on a claw *Tête de femme sur une griffe*
Tooktoo, Mina f 1937–
Poste-de-la-Baleine (Great Whale River)
1965
Dark green stone *Pierre vert foncé*
4 x 3.5 x 4

325

Human torso and head with antlers *Torse et tête humain avec des andouillers*
Simonee
Povungnituk
1953
Black stone *Pierre noire*
10 x 6 x 3.3

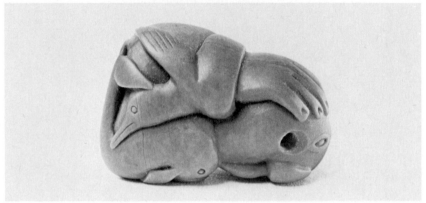

326
Pendant *Pendentif*
Napartuk, Henry 1932–
Poste-de-la-Baleine (Great Whale River)
1968
Grey-green stone *Pierre vert-de-gris*
4.5 x 3 x 2

327
Multiple image *Image composée*
Aupilarjuk, Mariano 1923–
Repulse Bay
1964
Dark grey stone *Pierre gris foncé*
15.5 x 8.5 x 8

328
Bird over man, man over all *Oiseau au-dessus d'homme, homme au-dessus de tout*
Artist unknown *Artiste inconnu*
Povungnituk or *ou* Inoucdjouac (Port Harrison)
1951
Grey stone *Pierre grise*
13 x 4 x 5.5

329
Spirit *Esprit*
Pirti, Levi Alasua 'Smith' 1926–
Povungnituk
1968
Dark grey stone *Pierre gris foncé*
10.5 x 8.5 x 10

330
Mother and child seated on human head *Mère et enfant assis sur une tête humaine*
Kaka 1928–
Cape Dorset
ca. 1955
Dark green stone *Pierre vert foncé*
15 x 11 x 8.5

331
Owl man *Homme hibou*
Tiktak 1916–
Rankin Inlet
1967
Black stone *Pierre noire*
27 X 12 X 14.5

332
Being *Etre*
Shimayook f 1924–
Cape Dorset
1967
Grey stone *Pierre grise*
14 x 12.5 x 9.5

333

Eskimo delousing a spirit *Homme épouillant un esprit*
Amittu, Davidialu Alasua (Davidealuk) 1910–
Povungnituk
ca. 1952
Black stone *Pierre noire*
18 x 20 x 10.5

334
Owl man *Homme hibou*
Latcholassie 1919–
Cape Dorset
1962
Green stone *Pierre verte*
19 X 21 X 7

335
Spirit *Esprit*
Kabubawakota 1928–
Cape Dorset
1967–68
Green stone *Pierre verte*
41 x 70 x 17

336
Mythological bird *Oiseau mythologique*
Amittu, Davidialu Alasua (Davidealuk) 1910–
Povungnituk
1958
Grey stone *Pierre grise*
44 x 39 x 16

337
Standing man *Homme debout*
Igjookhuak 1916–
Spence Bay
1969
Whale bone *Os de baleine*
57 x 47 x 28

338
Musk-ox with human face *Boeuf musqué à face humaine*
Tiktala, David 1927–
Baker Lake
ca. 1967
Black stone *Pierre noire*
29 X 43 X 19

339

Man standing on a seabird *Homme debout sur un oiseau de mer*
Ohaytok, Lucassie 1921–
Belcher Islands *Iles Belcher*
1959
Grey-green stone *Pierre vert-de-gris*
13 x 12 x 8

340

Dancing sea creature *Animal marin dansant*
Kiawak 1933–
Cape Dorset
1956
Green stone *Pierre verte*
15.5 x 10.5 x 10

341
Rabbit image *Image d'un lapin*
Jya (Yaw) 1930–
Cape Dorset
1957–58
Dark grey stone *Pierre gris foncé*
12.5 x 4 x 6

342

Sea goddess riding a seal *Déesse de la mer à cheval sur un phoque*
Niviaksiak 1908–1959
Cape Dorset
1958
Dark grey-green stone *Pierre vert-de-gris foncé*
9 x 19 x 7

343

Lemming carrying man *Lemming portant un homme*
Ashevak 1932–
Cape Dorset
1962–63
Green stone *Pierre verte*
14 X 34.5 X 9.5

344
Howling spirit (Tornrak) and its young *Esprit hurlant avec son petit*
Kiawak 1933–
Cape Dorset
1962
Green stone *Pierre verte*
24 X 22 X 11

345
Man dreaming of a seal *Homme rêvant à un phoque*
Angootikjuak, Kudloo f 1943–
Clyde River
1968
Green stone *Pierre verte*
21 x 13 x 22

346
Double man *Homme double*
Kavik, John 1897–
Rankin Inlet
1965
Dark grey stone *Pierre gris foncé*
25 x 7.5 x 8

347
Man riding strange dogs *Homme montant sur le dos de chiens étranges*
Markosie
Pangnirtung
1969
Whale bone *Os de baleine*
9.5 X 10.5 X 10.5

348
Spirit *Esprit*
Saggiak 1897–
Cape Dorset
1959
Bone *Os*
15.5 x 15 x 7

349

Male figure *Personnage masculin*
Dorset culture *Culture de Dorset*
Button Point site, SE tip of Bylot Island
Site de la Pointe Button, à l'extrémité sud-est de l'île Bylot
Wood *Bois*
11 X 4 X 10.5

350
Bear with spirit head *Ours à tête d'esprit*
Artist unknown *Artiste inconnu*
Black Lead Island *Ile Black Lead*
Before 1941 *Avant 1941*
Ivory *Ivoire*
2 x 6 x 1.5

351

Bears *Ours*
Artist unknown *Artiste inconnu*
Central Canadian Arctic *Arctique central du Canada*
Grey stone *Pierre grise*
3.5 x 5.5 x 1.5

352

Magic caribou *Caribou magique*
Tungilik, Mark 1913–
Repulse Bay
1951
Bone *Os*
15 x 7 x 6

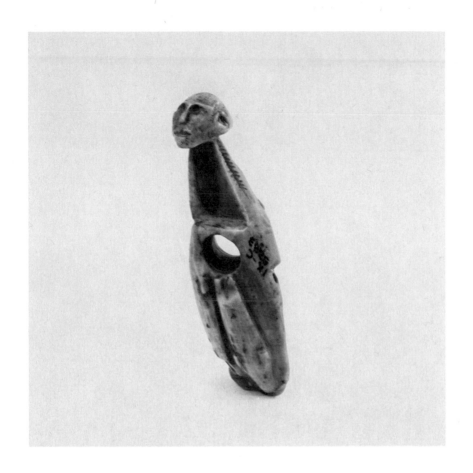

353
Effigy dragline handle *Poignée de ligne ornée d'une effigie*
Thule culture *Culture de Thulé*
Igloolik
Ivory *Ivoire*
1.6 x 5.8 x 1.5

354
Man and wolverine *Homme et carcajou*
Artist unknown *Artiste inconnu*
Eastern Canadian Arctic *Est de l'Arctique canadien*
Before 1914 *Avant 1914*
Ivory *Ivoire*
6 x 2.5 x 1.5

355
Spirit *Esprit*
Anaija 1913–
Spence Bay
1969
Whale bone *Os de baleine*
28 x 28 x 24

356

Needle case *Etui à aiguilles*
Dorset culture *Culture de Dorset*
Ivory *Ivoire*
9.3 x 3.8 x 2.4

357
Head *Tête*
Saggiak 1897–
Cape Dorset
1959
Bone *Os*
8 x 5.5 x 3

358
Man *Homme*
Artist unknown *Artiste inconnu*
Repulse Bay?
ca. 1955
Whale bone *Os de baleine*
10 x 6 x 4.5

359
Kneeling woman *Femme agenouillée*
Kavik, John 1897–
Rankin Inlet
1965
Grey stone *Pierre grise*
17.5 x 16 x 9.5

360
Group of heads *Groupe de têtes*
Tasseor, Lucy f 1934–
Eskimo Point
1967
Grey stone *Pierre grise*
9 x 15 x 8

361
Group of people *Groupe de personnes*
Arlutnar, Thérèse f 1926–
Eskimo Point
1968
Dark grey stone *Pierre gris foncé*
11.5 x 8 x 4.5

362
Face *Visage*
Dorset culture *Culture de Dorset*
Uvuguvik (20 miles sw of Cape Wolstenholme)
(20 milles au sud-ouest du cap Wolstenholme)
Ivory *Ivoire*
5.6 x 1.55 x 7

363

Faces *Visages*
Artist unknown *Artiste inconnu*
Prince of Wales Island *Ile Prince-de-Galles*
Before 1939 *Avant 1939*
Antler *Andouiller*
14 x 2.9 x 1

364
Woman *Femme*
Pangnark, John 1920–
Eskimo Point
1969
Black stone *Pierre noire*
11.5 X 7 X 14

365
Three faces and a duck *Trois visages et un canard*
Nuyaitok, Martha f 1944–
Repulse Bay
1967
Grey-green stone and antler *Pierre vert-de-gris et andouiller*
7 X 11 X 5

366
Head *Tête*
Nastapoka, Abraham 1900–
Inoucdjouac (Port Harrison)
1957
Dark green and orange stone *Pierre vert foncé et orange*
15.5 x 4.5 x 6

367
Head of a woman *Tête de femme*
Akeeah, Matthew 1940–
Baker Lake
1964
Black stone *Pierre noire*
8 x 5.5 x 3

368
Man *Homme*
Erkoolik, Toona 1935–
Baker Lake
1963
Black stone *Pierre noire*
19 x 16.5 x 11

369

Seated figure *Personnage assis*
Kupak, Felix 1918–
Repulse Bay
1969
Grey-green stone *Pierre vert-de-gris*
17 x 19 x 10.5

370
Man carrying two fish *Homme portant deux poissons*
Anigliak, Peterosee 1923–
Pangnirtung
ca. 1966
Whale bone *Os de baleine*
45 x 26 x 10.5

371
Human face with caribou antlers *Visage avec des andouillers de caribou*
Ugjuk, Thomas 1921–
Whale Cove
1966
Whale bone and antler *Os de baleine et andouiller*
43 X 22 X 23

372
Doll's face *Visage de poupée*
Kiawak 1933–
Cape Dorset
1960
Whale bone *Os de baleine*
13 X 12 X 3

373
Mask *Masque*
Artist unknown *Artiste inconnu*
Central Canadian Arctic *Arctique central du Canada*
Before 1927 *Avant 1927*
Wood *Bois*
20 x 18 x 7

374
Face *Visage*
Dorset culture *Culture de Dorset*
Mansel Island *Ile Mansel*
Bone *Os*
9 x 8 x 5.5

375
Faces *Visages*
Dorset culture *Culture de Dorset*
Igloolik area *Région d'Igloolik*
Caribou antler *Andouiller de caribou*
10 X 5.5 X 2.2

376
Masquette *Petit masque*
Dorset culture *Culture de Dorset*
Tyara site, Sugluk *Site de Tyara, Saglouc*
Ivory *Ivoire*
3.5 x 2 x 9

377
Face *Visage*
Dorset culture *Culture de Dorset*
Mansel Island *Ile Mansel*
Bone *Os*
5.4 x 3 x 0.6

378
Head *Tête*
Artist unknown *Artiste inconnu*
Povungnituk
ca. 1952
Black stone, bone and ivory *Pierre noire, os et ivoire*
9 x 8 x 8

379

Woman's head on base *Tête de femme sur sode*
Artist unknown *Artiste inconnu*
Baffin Island *Ile Baffin*
1952–53
Bone and human hair *Os et cheveux humains*
12 X 10 X 9

380

Harpoon head with face *Pointe de harpon ornée d'un visage*
Dorset culture *Culture de Dorset*
Igloolik area *Région d'Igloolik*
Walrus tusk *Défense de morse*
6 x 2 x 1.4

381

Man image *Représentation d'un homme*
Tiktak 1916–
Rankin Inlet
1961
Black stone *Pierre noire*
21 x 8.5 x 6

382

Face *Visage*
Dorset culture *Culture de Dorset*
Button Point site, SE tip of Bylot Island
Site de la Pointe Button, à l'extrémité sud-est de l'île Bylot
Wood *Bois*
11.7 X 1.7 X 0.9

383

Double face *Visage double*
Dorset culture *Culture de Dorset*
Buchanan site, south bank of Ekalluk River
Site de Buchanan, rive sud de la rivière Ekalluk
Bone *Os*
4.5 x 1.6 x 0.8

384

Unclean woman *Femme malpropre*
Koodluarlik, Kakasilala 1913–
Pangnirtung
1967–68
Whale bone, stone and antler *Os de baleine, pierre et andouiller*
35 x 66 x 22

385

Effigy drum handle *Manche de tambour avec effigie*
Artist unknown *Artiste inconnu*
Location unknown *Endroit inconnu*
Before 1903 *Avant 1903*
Bone *Os*
12 x 2.7 x 4

386

Two people *Deux personnes*
Kavik, John 1897–
Rankin Inlet
1965
Dark grey stone *Pierre gris foncé*
9.5 x 4 x 4.5

387

Two people *Deux personnes*
Ootnooyuk, Susan f 1918–
Eskimo Point
1968
Dark grey stone and beads *Pierre gris foncé et perles de verre*
12 x 6 x 4.5

388
Head *Tête*
Kallooar, Francis 1931–
Baker Lake
1964
Bone *Os*
10 x 4.5 x 6

389
Head *Tête*
Tikeayak, Eli 1933–
Rankin Inlet
1961
Black stone *Pierre noire*
17 x 8 x 3

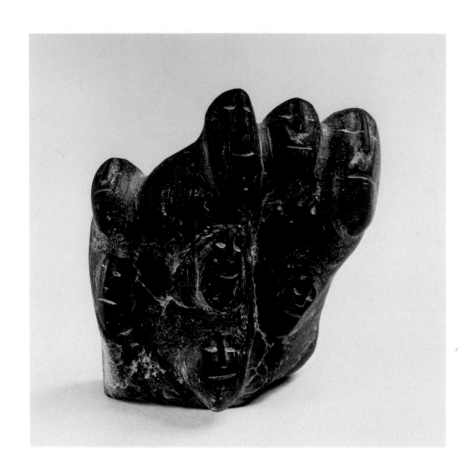

390
Group of figures *Groupe de personnages*
Tasseor, Lucy f 1934–
Eskimo Point
1969
Black stone *Pierre noire*
13.5 x 13.5 x 7

391
Man with raised arm *Homme avec un bras élevé*
Tikeayak, Eli 1933–
Rankin Inlet
ca. 1968
Dark grey stone *Pierre gris foncé*
10 x 7.5 x 3

392
Seated figure *Personnage assis*
Tudlik 1890–1962
Cape Dorset
1951
Black stone *Pierre noire*
8.5 x 3.5 x 5

393
Man *Homme*
Tasseor, Lucy f 1934–
Eskimo Point
1969
Black stone *Pierre noire*
11 x 7 x 4

394

Pointing man *Homme montrant du doigt*
Pangnark, John 1920–
Eskimo Point
1969
Black stone *Pierre noire*
10 x 9 x 3.5

395
Woman *Femme*
Pangnark, John 1920–
Eskimo Point
1969
Black stone *Pierre noire*
17 x 17 x 8.5

396
Man *Homme*
Pangnark, John 1920–
Eskimo Point
1969
Black stone *Pierre noire*
12 x 5 x 8

397

Kneeling man *Homme agenouillé*
Kavik, John 1897–
Rankin Inlet
1963
Black stone *Pierre noire*
9 x 7 x 7

398
Bust of a woman *Buste de femme*
Kudluk, Noah 1912–
Belcher Islands *Iles Belcher*
1954
Dark grey stone and ivory *Pierre gris foncé et ivoire*
21 X 14 X 12

399

Standing man, the King *Homme debout, le Roi*
Inukshuk, Peter 1896–
Baker Lake
1969
Black stone *Pierre noire*
22 x 13.5 x 8

400

Seated man *Homme assis*
Tiktak 1916–
Rankin Inlet
1963
Dark grey stone *Pierre gris foncé*
18 x 10.5 x 14

401

Bust of a woman *Buste de femme*
Tiktak 1916–
Rankin Inlet
1966–67
Grey stone *Pierre grise*
54 x 20 x 20

402
Bust of a woman *Buste de femme*
Kaka 1928–
Cape Dorset
1956
Dark grey stone *Pierre gris foncé*
22 x 24 x 14

403
Head *Tête*
Simaotik, Daniel 1907–1968
Inoucdjouac (Port Harrison)
1959–60
Black stone *Pierre noire*
20 x 16.5 x 19

404
Heads emerging from stone *Têtes sortant de la pierre*
Tiktak 1916–
Rankin Inlet
1967
Black stone *Pierre noire*
24 x 68 x 32

405
Man and bird *Homme et oiseau*
Kadojuak
Spence Bay
1969
Whale bone *Os de baleine*
62 x 67 x 17

Artists/Les artistes

Kupak, Felix 1918–
  369
Nuyaitok, Martha 1944–
  365
Piluardjuk 1901–
  145, 146
Qirluaq 1950–   174
Tartuk, Felicité 1924–
  254
Tungilik, Mark 1913–
  133, 352

SAGLOUC (SUGLUK)
Kulluaijuk, Uili 1946–
  116

Padlayat, Isaacie Qurquq 1934–
  289

SPENCE BAY
Anaija 1913–
  355
Igjookhuak 1916–
  337
Kadojuak 405

WHALE COVE
Miki (see Eskimo Point)
Ugjuk, Thomas 1921–
  110, 371

Lenders/Les prêteurs

Dr and Mrs A. C. Abbott, Winnipeg, Manitoba 170

A. Adamson, Winnipeg, Manitoba 210

The Bulman Collection, Winnipeg, Manitoba 254, 257

Mr and Mrs K. J. Butler, Baker Lake, Northwest Territories 102, 399

Mr and Mrs Ezio Cappadocia, Hamilton, Ontario 184, 195, 249, 255, 313, 315, 316, 332

Edgar Davidson, Montreal, Quebec 405

Jean-Paul Drolet, Ottawa, Ontario 107

Paul Duval, Toronto, Ontario 113, 209

W. Eccles, Toronto, Ontario 121, 238, 306

M. F. Feheley, Toronto, Ontario 158

Pat Furneaux, North Augusta, Ontario 215, 312

Mira Godard, Montreal, Quebec 262

N. E. Hallendy, Ottawa, Ontario 106, 369, 372, 401

Professor Elmer Harp, Jr, Hanover, New Hampshire, United States of America 63, 86

Dr and Mrs J. A. Hildes, Winnipeg, Manitoba 182

Margery Hinds, Ottawa, Ontario 240

Mr and Mrs Arthur A. Houghton Jr, New York, New York, United States of America 342, 344

Alma Houston, Ottawa, Ontario 193, 196, 197, 323, 392

James A. Houston, New York, New York, United States of America 266, 345, 347

Lilly Weil Jaffe, Vancouver, British Columbia 165

Mr and Mrs Harry Klamer, Toronto, Ontario 101, 155, 302

Ian Graham Lindsay, Ottawa, Ontario 124, 137, 212, 213, 325, 328, 378

Mr and Mrs L. Lippel, Montreal, Quebec 318

Dr and Mrs Luigi Logrippo, Kitchener, Ontario 394

Mr and Mrs Angus W. Murray, Winnipeg, Manitoba 139, 164, 265, 287, 289

Eugene B. Power, Ann Arbor, Michigan, United States of America 133, 231, 260, 341, 348, 357

Mr and Mrs Donald K. Reichert, Winnipeg, Manitoba 175

Mr and Mrs John K. B. Robertson, Ottawa, Ontario 117, 122, 179, 293, 296, 308, 403

J. Rousseau, Montreal, Quebec 153, 232, 250

Mr and Mrs T. P. Ryan, Cape Dorset, Northwest Territories 141, 142, 168, 190, 192, 204, 311

Mr and Mrs J. Shadbolt, Vancouver, British Columbia 187, 236, 274, 291

Mr and Mrs Fred Schaeffer, Thornhill, Ontario 355

Mr and Mrs Paul Schoeler, Ottawa, Ontario 152, 211

Dr and Mrs Morris C. Shumiatcher, Regina, Saskatchewan 105, 261

Mr and Mrs Lorne Smith, Winnipeg, Manitoba 178, 309

C. A. Stewart, Winnipeg, Manitoba 221

George Swinton, Winnipeg, Manitoba 103, 114, 159, 189, 247, 276, 299, 307, 317, 319, 321, 322, 327, 334, 346, 371, 381, 388, 397, 400

Dr William E. Taylor, Jr, Ottawa, Ontario 202

Vincent Tovell, Toronto, Ontario 157

Dr and Mrs Evan Turner, Philadelphia, Pennsylvania, United States of America 343, 367

Marcia Twomey, Winnipeg, Manitoba 201

Mr and Mrs A. M. Vansittart, Toronto, Ontario 384

Dennis Webster, Repulse Bay, Northwest Territories 288, 395

Professor and Mrs. R. G. Williamson, Rankin Inlet, Northwest Territories 223, 297, 331, 359, 386, 389

* Italic numbers indicate: collected
by Department of Indian Affairs and
Northern Development and deposited
with the National Museum of Man,
Ottawa.

Canadian Eskimo Arts Council

Design *Dessin*
ALLAN FLEMING
Printing *Impression*
HERZIG-SOMERVILLE LIMITED
Typography and binding *Typographie et reliure*
T. H. BEST PRINTING COMPANY LIMITED